FUTURESMITH

FUTURESMITH

Build Your Tomorrow with a Precise Today

JAMES ALLEN

Published by
Rupa Publications India Pvt. Ltd 2025
7/16, Ansari Road, Daryaganj
New Delhi 110002

Sales centres:
Bengaluru Chennai
Hyderabad Jaipur Kathmandu
Kolkata Mumbai Prayagraj

Edition copyright © Rupa Publications India Pvt. Ltd 2025

All rights reserved.
No part of this publication may be reproduced, transmitted,
or stored in a retrieval system, in any form or by any means,
electronic, mechanical, photocopying, recording or otherwise,
without the prior permission of the publisher.

P-ISBN: 978-93-6156-840-4
E-ISBN: 978-93-6156-981-4

First impression 2025

10 9 8 7 6 5 4 3 2 1

Printed in India

This book is sold subject to the condition that it shall not,
by way of trade or otherwise, be lent, resold, hired out, or otherwise
circulated, without the publisher's prior consent, in any form of
binding or cover other than that in which it is published.

Contents

Introduction   *vii*

1. Vision Crafting   1
2. Goal Setting Mastery   22
3. Time Management Techniques   39

PART ONE: THE MINDSET FOR SUCCESS

4. Developing a Growth Mindset   61
5. Daily Habits for Success   83
6. Embracing Change and Adaptability   105
7. Building Strong Relationships   122
8. Financial Planning for the Future   142

PART TWO: WHOLESOMENESS AND WELLNESS CARE

9. Health and Wellness   171
10. Leveraging Technology for Productivity   186
11. Overcoming Obstacles and Resilience   193

PART THREE: LIFELONG LEARNING AND LEGACY

12. Continuous Learning and Skill Development   203
13. Ethical Living and Social Responsibility   214
14. Creating a Legacy   223

Introduction

Futuresmithing is an intricate, deliberate, and thoughtful process where one meticulously shapes and crafts one's future through precise and intentional actions taken in the present. The term itself conjures images of an artisan, much like a blacksmith, who skillfully moulds and shapes metal into a desired form. This vivid metaphor encapsulates the essence of futuresmithing: a delicate and deliberate art form where each action, much like each hammer strike, contributes to the overall creation of a beautifully crafted future.

A blacksmith approaches their craft with a blend of strength, precision, and artistry, understanding that each blow of the hammer, each turn of the metal, and each moment of heat application is critical to the final product. Similarly, a futuresmith approaches their life with an understanding that every action, decision, and habit is instrumental in shaping their future. *The futuresmith knows that the future is forged in the fires of the present, and thus, they give careful attention to every detail of their current actions.*

Unlike the simplistic notion of goal-setting, futuresmithing transcends this idea by embodying a comprehensive and holistic approach to personal and professional growth. Goal-setting often involves identifying a target and working towards it, but futuresmithing encompasses a broader, more integrated perspective. *It's about recognizing that our lives are not compartmentalized into isolated goals but are a cohesive blend of various aspects—emotional, physical, mental, and social.*

The concept of futuresmithing emphasizes the profound

interconnectedness of our daily actions and their cumulative long-term impact. *It's an understanding that every small decision, whether it's choosing to read a book instead of watching television, eating a healthy meal instead of junk food, or spending time with loved ones instead of isolating oneself, has a ripple effect on our future.* These seemingly insignificant choices accumulate over time, creating a substantial impact on the trajectory of our lives. Futuresmithing is about being aware of this interconnectedness and making choices that align with our desired future.

Futuresmithing is not merely about setting aspirations or achieving milestones but about fostering a continuous journey of self-improvement and mindful living. *It's about understanding that life is a constant evolution, and there is always room for growth and development.* Mindful living plays a crucial role in this journey, as it involves being present and fully engaged in each moment, making deliberate choices that align with our long-term goals.

Embracing the Role of a Futuresmith

To embrace the role of a futuresmith, one must cultivate a deep sense of awareness and intentionality. This involves regularly reflecting on one's actions and their alignment with personal values and long-term goals. *It also means being proactive in making necessary adjustments and being resilient in the face of challenges.* A futuresmith views setbacks not as failures but as opportunities for growth and learning. They understand that the path to their desired future is not always straightforward but requires perseverance, adaptability, and a positive outlook.

Futuresmithing requires a comprehensive approach to personal and professional growth. This involves setting clear and meaningful goals, developing a strategic plan to achieve them, and continuously monitoring progress. It also means paying attention to all aspects of one's life, including health, relationships, career, and personal development. By taking a holistic approach, a futuresmith ensures that growth is balanced and sustainable, avoiding the pitfalls of focusing too narrowly on one area at the expense of others.

The Core Philosophy of Futuresmithing

At its very core, the philosophy of futuresmithing is built upon a profound recognition that the future is not a distant, abstract concept existing in a realm beyond our immediate reach. Rather, it is a direct and tangible result of the actions we undertake in the present moment. *This fundamental understanding shifts our perspective from a passive expectation of what is to come to an active and dynamic engagement with the here and now.* Futuresmithing posits that the future is continually being forged through our current decisions, behaviours, and habits, shaping the trajectory of our lives in profound ways.

The Future as a Tangible Outcome of Present Actions

The notion that the future is a tangible outcome of present actions is a cornerstone of futuresmithing. It underscores the importance of recognizing that every choice we make, no matter how small, contributes to the formation of our future. This perspective challenges the conventional view of the future as an uncertain and distant possibility, bringing it into the realm of immediate influence and control. By understanding that our daily actions have long-term implications, we become more intentional and deliberate in our choices, aiming to align them with our desired outcomes.

Embracing a Mindset of Constant Self-Awareness

Futuresmithing urges individuals to adopt a mindset of constant self-awareness. *This involves cultivating a deep and continuous awareness of our thoughts, emotions, and actions, and understanding how they influence our overall trajectory.* Self-awareness is the foundation upon which futuresmithing is built, as it enables us to recognize patterns in our behaviours, identify areas for improvement, and make conscious adjustments to align with our long-term goals. This heightened state of awareness allows us to navigate life's challenges with greater clarity and purpose, ensuring that our actions are always in harmony with our aspirations.

Strategic Planning for Long-Term Goals

Strategic planning is another critical component of the futuresmithing philosophy. It involves setting clear, specific, and achievable long-term goals and developing a comprehensive plan to attain them. This process requires a deep understanding of our values, priorities, and aspirations, as well as a realistic assessment of our current circumstances and resources. By engaging in strategic planning, we create a roadmap that guides our actions and decisions, helping us stay focused and motivated even in the face of obstacles and setbacks.

The Perpetual Process of Refinement

The journey of futuresmithing is characterised by a perpetual process of refinement. It is not a one-time effort but an ongoing commitment to self-improvement and growth. This process involves regularly evaluating our progress, reflecting on our experiences, and making necessary adjustments to stay on course. *It requires a willingness to learn from our mistakes, adapt to changing circumstances, and continuously strive for excellence.* By embracing this continuous cycle of reflection and refinement, we ensure that our actions remain aligned with our long-term goals, and we stay on the path toward our desired future.

Thoughts, Behaviours, and Decisions

At the heart of futuresmithing is the alignment of our thoughts, behaviours, and decisions with our long-term goals. This alignment is essential for achieving a coherent and fulfilling life. It involves cultivating positive and empowering thought patterns that support our aspirations, developing habits and behaviours that contribute to our growth, and making decisions that reflect our values and priorities. By ensuring that our internal and external actions are in harmony, we create a sense of congruence and integrity that propels us toward our future with confidence and purpose.

Commitment

A key aspect of the futuresmithing philosophy is the commitment to continuous growth. This involves an unwavering dedication to personal and professional development, seeking out opportunities to learn, grow, and evolve. It requires a proactive approach to life, where we actively pursue knowledge, skills, and experiences that enhance our capabilities and broaden our horizons. *By embracing a growth mindset, we become more resilient, adaptable, and open to new possibilities, ensuring that we are always moving forward on our journey toward our goals.*

Intentional Living

Futuresmithing emphasizes the power of intentional living. It encourages us to live with purpose and mindfulness, making deliberate choices that reflect our values and aspirations. Intentional living involves being fully present in each moment, understanding the significance of our actions, and taking responsibility for the outcomes we create. *By living intentionally,* we cultivate a sense of agency and empowerment, knowing that we have the ability to shape our future through the actions we take today.

The Holistic Approach to Growth

Futuresmithing requires an unwavering commitment to personal and professional development. This commitment is not limited to any single aspect of life but rather embraces a holistic view of growth, where every facet of life is interconnected and equally significant. The essence of this approach lies in the understanding that one cannot simply focus on career achievements while neglecting personal well-being, or vice versa. A truly effective futuresmith integrates all aspects of their life—physical, mental, emotional, and social—into a cohesive strategy aimed at continuous improvement.

Embracing a Comprehensive View of Development

To fully grasp the holistic approach to growth, one must recognize that human beings are complex and multifaceted. Our lives are composed of various interconnected dimensions, each influencing and being influenced by the others. For instance, physical health affects mental clarity, emotional stability influences social interactions, and professional success impacts personal satisfaction. By acknowledging these interconnections, a futuresmith adopts a comprehensive view of development, ensuring that no single aspect of life is overlooked or undervalued.

Physical Well-Being

Physical well-being is a foundational element of holistic growth. It involves maintaining a healthy body through regular exercise, balanced nutrition, adequate rest, and preventive healthcare. A futuresmith understands that physical health is crucial for overall well-being and optimal performance in other areas of life. Therefore, they prioritise activities and habits that promote physical fitness and vitality, recognizing that a strong and healthy body provides the energy and resilience needed to pursue long-term goals.

Mental Clarity and Cognitive Growth

Mental clarity and cognitive growth are essential components of the holistic approach. This dimension focuses on nurturing the mind through continuous learning, critical thinking, and intellectual stimulation. A futuresmith engages in activities that challenge and expand their cognitive abilities, such as reading, studying, problem-solving, and engaging in meaningful conversations. By fostering mental growth, they enhance their capacity for creativity, innovation, and strategic planning, all of which are vital for shaping a successful future.

Cultivating Emotional Intelligence

Emotional intelligence is another key aspect of holistic growth. It involves understanding and managing one's emotions, as well as recognizing and empathizing with the emotions of others. A futuresmith cultivates emotional intelligence by developing self-awareness, practising emotional regulation, and building strong interpersonal relationships. This emotional competence enables them to navigate life's challenges with resilience, maintain healthy relationships, and create a supportive social network that contributes to overall well-being.

Building Strong Social Connections

Social connections are integral to a holistic approach to growth. Human beings are inherently social creatures, and our interactions with others play a significant role in our happiness and fulfilment.

A futuresmith prioritises building and maintaining strong, positive relationships with family, friends, colleagues, and the community. These relationships provide emotional support, opportunities for collaboration, and a sense of belonging, all of which are essential for a balanced and enriched life.

Balancing Personal and Professional Life

A central tenet of the holistic approach to growth is the balance between personal and professional life. A futuresmith recognizes that excelling in one area at the expense of another leads to imbalances that can undermine overall well-being and long-term success. Therefore, they strive to achieve harmony between their career ambitions and personal fulfilment. This balance involves setting boundaries, managing time effectively, and prioritising activities that align with both personal values and professional goals.

Creating a Cohesive Growth Strategy

To effectively integrate all aspects of life into a cohesive growth strategy, a futuresmith develops a comprehensive plan that outlines specific goals and actions for each dimension of life. This strategy is dynamic and adaptable, allowing for adjustments as circumstances change and new opportunities arise. By regularly reviewing and refining this plan, a futuresmith ensures that their growth remains aligned with their evolving aspirations and life circumstances.

Commitment to Continuous Improvement

The holistic approach to growth is characterised by an unwavering commitment to continuous improvement. It requires a mindset that embraces lifelong learning, self-reflection, and proactive adaptation. A futuresmith is always seeking ways to enhance their well-being, performance, and overall quality of life. This commitment involves setting challenging but achievable goals, celebrating progress, and learning from setbacks. By maintaining this dedication to growth, a futuresmith ensures that their journey is marked by constant evolution and sustained success.

Mindfulness and Strategic Planning

A futuresmith's journey is marked by mindfulness and strategic planning. Mindfulness involves a heightened awareness of the present moment, enabling individuals to make conscious choices that align with their desired future. This level of awareness helps in identifying and eliminating detrimental habits while fostering positive ones that propel them towards their goals.

Strategic planning, on the other hand, involves setting a clear and detailed vision of what one wants to achieve. This vision acts as a guiding star, helping to chart the course and navigate through life's uncertainties. With a well-defined vision, a futuresmith can break down their long-term objectives into manageable, actionable steps, ensuring steady progress towards their aspirations.

Commitment to Continuous Self-Improvement

The journey of futuresmithing is underpinned by an unwavering commitment to continuous self-improvement. It's a dynamic process that involves regular reflection, evaluation, and adaptation. A futuresmith regularly assesses their progress, learns from their experiences, and adjusts their strategies to stay on course. This relentless pursuit of excellence ensures that they are constantly evolving and moving closer to their ultimate goals.

The Interconnectedness of Actions and Long-Term Impact

Every action taken today has a ripple effect on the future. This understanding is central to the philosophy of futuresmithing. By recognizing the long-term impact of their present actions, a futuresmith makes informed decisions that contribute positively to their future. This interconnectedness underscores the importance of living intentionally, with a clear awareness of how today's choices shape tomorrow's reality.

The Vision of Achievements and Steadfast Dedication

A futuresmith's mindset is characterised by a clear and compelling vision of what they want to achieve. This vision serves as both motivation and direction, providing the clarity needed to pursue their goals with passion and purpose. Alongside this vision, a futuresmith exhibits steadfast dedication to the necessary actions and disciplines required to realize their dreams. This dedication involves perseverance, resilience, and an unwavering focus on the end goal, despite any challenges or setbacks encountered along the way.

The Importance of Precise Actions Today for a Better Tomorrow

In the journey of futuresmithing, the actions we take today hold significant weight. These actions, whether small or large, create ripples that influence our future circumstances. This principle is rooted in the law of cause and effect, which states that every cause (action) has a corresponding effect (result). By understanding and leveraging this law, we can shape our future outcomes more predictably and positively.

Taking precise actions means being intentional and thoughtful about every decision. It involves setting clear, achievable goals and breaking them down into manageable steps. Each step should be executed with purpose and care, ensuring that it aligns with the larger vision. This process requires discipline, consistency, and a proactive mindset.

For example, consider the goal of achieving financial independence. This objective cannot be attained overnight but through a series of calculated and deliberate actions: saving a portion of one's income, investing wisely, seeking financial education, and avoiding unnecessary debts. Each of these actions contributes incrementally to the larger goal, illustrating the power of precise actions in shaping a desirable future.

Moreover, the practice of precise actions fosters a sense of control and empowerment. When we take charge of our actions, we become active participants in our destiny rather than passive observers. This shift in mindset can lead to increased motivation, resilience, and a greater sense of fulfilment.

Overview of the Book's Structure and Objectives

"Futuresmith: Build Your Tomorrow with a Precise Today" is designed to guide readers through the process of futuresmithing, providing practical tools, insights, and inspiration to craft a better future. The book is structured to address various aspects of personal and professional development, each chapter building upon the last to create a comprehensive roadmap for success.

This book is like a GPS for your future, guiding you to take all the right turns today so you don't end up lost on Wacky Street tomorrow. Packed with practical advice, real-life tales of triumph, and step-by-step instructions, it's like a choose-your-own-adventure book for grown-ups. Whether you're aiming for career superstardom, relationship ninja status, financial wizardry, or just a life that doesn't feel like a Monday morning, this book equips you with the tools and wisdom to start sculpting your future without needing a crystal ball or a time machine. It's like having a cheat code for life, but without the guilt of cheating - win-win!

1

Vision Crafting

"Cherish your visions; cherish your ideals; cherish the music that stirs in your heart, the beauty that forms in your mind, the loveliness that drapes your purest thoughts for out of them will grow all delightful conditions, all heavenly environment; of these if you but remain true to them your world will at last be built."

Visions are the blueprints of our future. They are the vivid pictures we paint in our minds about what we desire to achieve and become. Cherishing these visions means nurturing and protecting them, allowing them to flourish and guide our actions. Your vision is your promise of what you shall one day be; your ideal is the prophecy of what you shall at last unveil. The power of a clear vision cannot be overstated, as it provides direction, motivation, and a sense of purpose.

Techniques to Define Personal and Professional Visions

1. Self-Reflection and Awareness

Identify Your Passions:

What activities make you feel most alive and fulfilled? Your passions often point to your core values and can help define your vision.

Assess Your Strengths and Weaknesses:

Understanding your strengths can help you leverage them in your vision, while acknowledging your weaknesses allows you to plan for improvement.

Reflect on Your Past Experiences:

Consider the moments when you felt most successful or content. What were you doing? Who were you with? These reflections can provide valuable insights into your vision.

Analyse Your Values and Beliefs:

Your vision should align with your core values and beliefs. These are the principles that guide your decisions and actions. Understanding what matters most to you will help ensure that your vision is meaningful and sustainable.

Envision Your Legacy:

Think about the impact you want to leave on the world. What do you want to be remembered for? This can provide a long-term perspective and help you define a vision that goes beyond personal success to include contributions to society.

2. Visualization Techniques

Mental Imagery:

Spend time each day visualizing your desired future. Imagine the details vividly – where you are, what you are doing, who you are with, and how you feel.

Vision Boards:

Create a physical or digital collage of images, words, and quotes that represent your vision. Place it somewhere you will see it daily to reinforce your goals.

Written Descriptions:

Write a detailed description of your ideal life in the present tense, as if it is already happening. This exercise can help solidify your vision in your mind.

Guided Visualization Meditations:

Participate in guided meditations focused on envisioning your future. These meditations can help you relax, clear your mind, and focus on your goals. Many resources are available online or through apps that can assist with this practice.

Future Self Exercises:

Write letters from your future self, detailing the achievements and milestones you have reached. This can help you clarify your vision and identify the steps needed to get there. Reflect on the advice and encouragement your future self might offer.

Create a Storyboard:

Draw or sketch a storyboard that outlines the key events and milestones in your journey towards your vision. This visual narrative can help you see the progression and keep you motivated.

3. Goal Setting and Planning

Set SMART Goals:

Ensure your goals are Specific, Measurable, Achievable, Relevant, and Time-bound. These criteria help make your vision actionable.

Break Down Goals:

Divide your long-term vision into smaller, manageable goals. Create a timeline for achieving these goals, with milestones to track your progress.

Create an Action Plan:

Develop a step-by-step plan to achieve your goals. Include specific actions, resources needed, and potential obstacles with contingency plans.

Prioritise Your Goals:

Determine which goals are most important and tackle them first. Prioritising helps you allocate your time and resources effectively. Consider the impact and feasibility of each goal to establish a clear order of priorities.

Review and Adjust Regularly:

Periodically review your goals and action plans to ensure they remain aligned with your vision. Be open to making adjustments as needed. Flexibility is key to adapting to changes and staying on course.

Celebrate Milestones:

Acknowledge and celebrate your achievements along the way. Recognizing your progress can boost your motivation and confidence. Take time to reflect on how far you have come and the lessons learned.

4. Seek Inspiration and Mentorship

Learn from Others:

Study the lives of people who have achieved similar visions. Read biographies, watch interviews, and learn from their experiences.

Find a Mentor:

Seek guidance from someone who has already achieved what you aspire to. A mentor can provide valuable insights, support, and accountability.

Join Communities and Networks:

Connect with like-minded individuals who share your vision or aspirations. Being part of a supportive community can provide encouragement, resources, and opportunities for collaboration.

Attend Workshops and Seminars:

Participate in events that focus on personal and professional development. These can offer new perspectives, skills, and motivation to pursue your vision.

Engage with Online Resources:

Explore blogs, podcasts, webinars, and online courses related to your vision. There is a wealth of information available that can help you refine your goals and strategies.

5. Stay Flexible and Adaptable

Embrace Change:

Understand that your vision may evolve over time. Stay open to new opportunities and be willing to adjust your goals as needed. Flexibility allows you to adapt to changing circumstances and continue moving forward.

Reflect and Reassess:

Regularly review your vision and progress. Reflect on what is working and what is not, and make adjustments to stay on track. Continuous evaluation helps ensure that your efforts remain aligned with your vision.

Develop Resilience:

Cultivate the ability to bounce back from setbacks and challenges. Resilience is essential for maintaining momentum and staying committed to your vision.

Stay Curious and Open-Minded:

Be open to new ideas, experiences, and perspectives. Curiosity can lead to innovative solutions and opportunities that align with your vision.

Balance Planning with Flexibility:

While having a detailed plan is important, be prepared to adapt and pivot when necessary. Finding the right balance between planning and flexibility is key to navigating the journey towards your vision.

Historical Perspectives on Vision Crafting

The Role of Vision in Ancie/nt Civilizations

In ancient civilizations, vision and foresight were often attributed to leaders, prophets, and sages. These individuals were revered for their ability to see beyond the present and guide their communities towards a better future. Vision crafting played a crucial role in shaping societies and influencing the course of history.

The Vision of Alexander the Great:

Alexander the Great envisioned a vast empire that would unite diverse cultures and peoples. His vision of a Hellenistic world influenced his military strategies and administrative policies. Through his conquests, Alexander spread Greek culture and ideas, leaving a lasting legacy.

The Vision of Confucius:

Confucius envisioned a society based on harmony, morality, and respect for tradition. His teachings emphasized the importance of education, family values, and ethical leadership. Confucius' vision has had a profound impact on Chinese culture and philosophy for centuries.

The Vision of Socrates:

Socrates envisioned a world where individuals pursued knowledge and truth through questioning and dialogue. His vision of intellectual inquiry and critical thinking laid the foundation for Western philosophy and education.

The Vision of Akhenaten:

Pharaoh Akhenaten of ancient Egypt envisioned a monotheistic religion centred around the worship of Aten, the sun disk. His vision led to significant religious reforms and the establishment of a new capital city, Amarna. Although his vision was short-lived, it left an enduring mark on Egyptian history.

Visionary Leaders in History

Leonardo da Vinci:

Leonardo da Vinci's vision extended beyond art to encompass science, engineering, and anatomy. His notebooks are filled with visionary ideas and inventions, many of which were ahead of his time. Leonardo's ability to envision possibilities in multiple disciplines made him a quintessential Renaissance man.

Galileo Galilei:

Galileo's vision of a heliocentric universe challenged the prevailing geocentric model. His observations and experiments laid the groundwork for modern astronomy and physics. Despite facing opposition from the Church, Galileo remained committed to his vision of scientific discovery.

Martin Luther King Jr.:

Dr. Martin Luther King Jr. envisioned a society where people of all races could live together in harmony and equality. His vision of civil rights and social justice inspired the American Civil Rights Movement and continues to influence global struggles for human rights.

Mother Teresa:

Mother Teresa's vision was to serve the poorest of the poor and provide care for those in need. Her unwavering dedication to her vision led to the establishment of the Missionaries of Charity, an organisation that continues to provide humanitarian aid worldwide.

Philosophical Insights on Vision Crafting

The Power of Imagination

Philosophers throughout history have emphasized the importance of imagination in vision crafting. Imagination allows individuals to transcend the limitations of their current circumstances and envision new possibilities.

Immanuel Kant:

Kant believed that imagination plays a crucial role in shaping human experience and understanding. He argued that imagination bridges the gap between sensory perception and conceptual thought, enabling individuals to create and interpret meaning.

Jean-Paul Sartre:

Sartre's existentialist philosophy highlights the role of imagination in creating meaning and purpose in life. According to Sartre, individuals have the freedom to imagine and choose their own paths, shaping their existence through their visions and actions.

Henry David Thoreau:

Thoreau's philosophy of transcendentalism emphasizes the power of individual vision and self-reliance. He advocated for living authentically and pursuing one's true passions, as expressed in his famous work, "Walden."

Friedrich Nietzsche:

Nietzsche's concept of the "Übermensch" (Overman) embodies the idea of visionary individuals who transcend conventional limitations and create their own values. He believed that such individuals have the power to shape the future through their visionary ideals.

CASE STUDIES OF SUCCESSFUL VISIONARIES

Elon Musk: The Visionary Entrepreneur

Vision: Elon Musk's vision includes reducing the risk of human extinction by making life multiplanetary, revolutionizing transportation through electric vehicles, and creating sustainable energy solutions.

Techniques: Musk uses a combination of grand vision, relentless work ethic, and strategic goal setting. He visualizes his goals clearly and breaks them down into actionable steps, continually innovating and adapting.

Outcome: Musk's companies, such as SpaceX, Tesla, and SolarCity, have made significant advancements in space travel, electric vehicles, and solar energy, respectively.

Detailed Analysis:

Elon Musk's vision for a multiplanetary future began with his fascination with space exploration. He founded SpaceX with the goal of reducing the cost of space travel and eventually establishing a human colony on Mars. Through innovative engineering and a focus on reusable rockets, SpaceX has achieved milestones such as the successful launch and landing of the Falcon 9 rocket and the development of the Starship spacecraft.

In the automotive industry, Musk's vision for sustainable transportation led to the creation of Tesla, a company dedicated to producing electric vehicles. Tesla's advancements in battery technology, autonomous driving, and energy storage have revolutionized the industry and accelerated the transition to sustainable energy.

Oprah Winfrey: The Media Mogul

Background: Oprah Winfrey overcame a difficult childhood marked by poverty, abuse, and discrimination. Despite these challenges, she pursued education and a career in media.

Resilience: Winfrey's resilience was evident in her determination to succeed and her ability to turn adversity into opportunity. She used her platform to inspire and empower others.

Vision: Oprah Winfrey envisioned a life of influence, empowering people through media and philanthropy.

Techniques: Oprah utilized self-reflection to understand her passions and strengths. She set clear goals, built a strong personal brand, and consistently visualized her success.

Outcome: Oprah became one of the most influential media personalities in the world, building a multimedia empire and using her platform to inspire and uplift others.

Detailed Analysis:

Oprah Winfrey's vision for empowerment and influence began with her passion for storytelling and connecting with people. She leveraged her strengths in communication and empathy to create "The Oprah Winfrey Show," a groundbreaking talk show that addressed a wide range of social issues and personal stories.

Oprah's commitment to her vision extended beyond television. She founded the Oprah Winfrey Network (OWN), launched a successful magazine, and established the Oprah Winfrey Leadership Academy for Girls in South Africa. Her philanthropic efforts and advocacy for education and women's rights have made a lasting impact on countless lives.

Mahatma Gandhi: The Leader of Nonviolent Resistance

Vision: Gandhi's vision was to achieve India's independence from British rule through nonviolent resistance and to promote social and economic reforms.

Techniques: Gandhi's approach included deep self-reflection, spiritual practices, and unwavering commitment to his ideals. He inspired millions through his actions and speeches, setting clear goals and strategies for civil disobedience.

Outcome: Gandhi's leadership played a crucial role in India's independence, and his principles of nonviolence and civil rights continue to influence global movements for justice and equality.

Detailed Analysis:

Mahatma Gandhi's vision for nonviolent resistance, or "Satyagraha," was rooted in his belief in truth and justice. He led numerous campaigns against British colonial rule, including the Salt March and the Quit India Movement, mobilizing millions of Indians to participate in acts of civil disobedience.

Gandhi's vision extended to social and economic reforms, including the promotion of self-reliance, rural development, and communal harmony. His commitment to nonviolence and ethical leadership set a powerful example for future leaders and movements around the world.

J.K. Rowling: The Author of Harry Potter

Background: J.K. Rowling faced numerous rejections from publishers before the Harry Potter series was accepted. She also experienced personal hardships, including financial struggles and a difficult divorce.

Resilience: Rowling's resilience was evident in her perseverance and dedication to her craft. She continued writing despite setbacks and rejections.

Vision: J.K. Rowling envisioned creating a magical world that would captivate readers and inspire their imagination.

Techniques: Rowling used visualization and detailed planning, meticulously outlining her story before writing. Despite numerous rejections, she remained committed to her vision.

Outcome: The Harry Potter series became a global phenomenon, transforming Rowling's life and impacting millions of readers worldwide.

Detailed Analysis:

J.K. Rowling's vision for the Harry Potter series began as a simple idea that grew into a richly detailed world of magic and adventure. She spent years developing the characters, plot, and lore of the series, demonstrating remarkable persistence and creativity.

Rowling's ability to visualize her stories vividly and plan them meticulously allowed her to create a coherent and engaging narrative. Her vision not only brought her personal success but also inspired a new generation of readers and writers, leaving a lasting legacy in the world of literature.

Nelson Mandela: The Anti-Apartheid Revolutionary

Vision: Nelson Mandela's vision was to end apartheid in South Africa and establish a multiracial democracy.

Techniques: Mandela demonstrated resilience, strategic planning, and unwavering commitment to justice. He visualized a free and equal South Africa, using his influence to inspire others.

Outcome: Mandela's efforts culminated in the dismantling of apartheid and his election as South Africa's first black president, symbolizing a new era of equality and justice.

Detailed Analysis:

Nelson Mandela's vision for a democratic and inclusive South Africa was driven by his deep sense of justice and equality. Despite spending 27 years in prison, Mandela remained steadfast in his commitment to nonviolent resistance and reconciliation.

Mandela's leadership during the negotiations to end apartheid and his efforts to promote unity and forgiveness set the foundation for a peaceful transition to democracy. His vision and actions continue to inspire global movements for human rights and social justice.

THE ROLE OF TECHNOLOGY IN VISION CRAFTING

Digital Tools for Vision Crafting

Vision Crafting Apps:

Explore apps designed to help you visualize and achieve your goals. These apps can provide guided visualizations, goal tracking, and motivational resources.

Online Vision Board Platforms:

Utilize digital platforms to create and share vision boards. These platforms offer templates, inspiration, and tools to make your vision board interactive and accessible.

Virtual Reality (VR) Visualization:

VR technology allows you to immerse yourself in a virtual representation of your desired future. This immersive experience can make your vision more tangible and motivating.

Productivity and Planning Software:

Use software tools for project management, goal setting, and time tracking. These tools can help you organise your vision into actionable steps and monitor your progress.

Vision Crafting in Different Cultures

Cultural Perspectives on Vision and Foresight

Indigenous Wisdom:

Many indigenous cultures emphasize the importance of vision and foresight in their traditions and practices. Learn from their holistic approaches to vision crafting and community well-being.

Eastern Philosophies:

Explore how vision crafting is integrated into Eastern philosophies such as Taoism, Buddhism, and Hinduism. These philosophies often emphasize balance, mindfulness, and interconnectedness.

Western Traditions:

Examine the role of vision in Western traditions, from ancient Greek philosophy to contemporary personal development. Western approaches often highlight individualism, innovation, and progress.

African Visionary Practices:

Discover the visionary practices of African cultures, including the role of storytelling, ancestors, and communal visioning in shaping the future.

THE PSYCHOLOGY OF VISION CRAFTING

Cognitive and Emotional Aspects

The Neuroscience of Vision:

Understand how the brain processes vision and imagination. Explore the neural mechanisms that enable visualization and goal setting.

Emotional Intelligence:

Learn how emotional intelligence impacts vision crafting. Developing self-awareness, empathy, and emotional regulation can enhance your ability to achieve your vision.

Motivation and Self-Determination:

Examine theories of motivation and self-determination. Understanding intrinsic and extrinsic motivators can help you sustain your efforts towards your vision.

Positive Psychology:

Incorporate principles of positive psychology to enhance your well-being and resilience. Practices such as gratitude, mindfulness, and strengths-based approaches can support your vision.

Inspirational Leadership:

Develop the ability to inspire and motivate others with your vision. Learn how to communicate your vision compellingly and authentically.

Strategic Thinking:

Cultivate strategic thinking skills to align your vision with practical actions. Effective leaders balance visionary ideas with concrete plans and adaptability.

Empathy and Inclusivity:

Foster empathy and inclusivity in your leadership approach. A visionary leader values diverse perspectives and creates an environment where everyone feels heard and valued.

Resilience and Perseverance:

Build resilience and perseverance to navigate challenges and setbacks. Visionary leaders demonstrate unwavering commitment to their vision despite obstacles.

FUTURE TRENDS IN VISION CRAFTING

Emerging Trends and Innovations

Artificial Intelligence (AI) and Vision Crafting:

Explore how AI technologies can support vision crafting. AI tools can provide personalized insights, predictive analytics, and adaptive learning experiences.

Sustainability and Visioning:

Examine the growing importance of sustainability in vision crafting. Future visions increasingly emphasize environmental stewardship, social responsibility, and long-term well-being.

Global Collaboration:

Understand the role of global collaboration in vision crafting. The interconnectedness of the modern world offers opportunities for collective visioning and shared solutions to global challenges.

Ethical Considerations:

Consider the ethical implications of your vision. Reflect on how your vision aligns with values such as justice, equity, and respect for all beings.

PERSONAL REFLECTIONS AND JOURNALING PROMPTS

Deepening Your Vision Crafting Practice

Reflective Journaling:

Use journaling prompts to deepen your self-reflection and awareness. Regularly writing about your vision, goals, and experiences can provide clarity and insight.

Gratitude Journals:

Keep a gratitude journal to cultivate a positive mindset. Reflecting on what you are grateful for can enhance your well-being and support your vision.

Mindfulness Practices:

Integrate mindfulness practices into your daily routine. Mindfulness can help you stay present, reduce stress, and maintain focus on your vision.

Vision Check-Ins:

Schedule regular check-ins with yourself to review your vision and progress. Reflect on your achievements, challenges, and adjustments needed to stay on course.

VISION CRAFTING AND PERSONAL GROWTH

The Lifelong Journey of Vision Crafting

Embracing Lifelong Learning:

Commit to continuous learning and growth. Stay curious and

open to new experiences, knowledge, and skills that can enrich your vision.

Personal Development Plans:

Create a personal development plan that aligns with your vision. Identify areas for growth, set development goals, and seek opportunities for learning and improvement.

Balancing Ambition and Contentment:

Find a balance between pursuing ambitious goals and appreciating the present moment. Cultivate contentment and gratitude alongside your drive for achievement.

Legacy and Impact:

Reflect on the legacy you want to leave and the impact you want to make. Consider how your vision contributes to the well-being of others and the world.

Final Thoughts

Crafting a vision is not merely a foundational step in the journey of futuresmithing; it is the **very bedrock upon which the edifice of your future is built**. Vision crafting is an intricate and dynamic process that demands a deep engagement with your innermost passions, values, and aspirations. Through this profound engagement, you begin to see the contours of your future taking shape, guided by the light of your most cherished dreams and ideals.

By cherishing your visions, you are nurturing the seeds of your future. These visions, often born from the depths of your heart and soul, require careful cultivation and unwavering commitment. They are the **sparks that ignite your journey**, providing a sense of direction and purpose that propels you forward. Your visions are not static; they are living entities that grow and evolve as you do. By remaining true to them, you ensure they remain vibrant and robust, capable of guiding you through life's complexities and challenges.

Defining clear goals is the next critical step in this transformative journey. Goals act as the milestones marking your progress toward realizing your vision. They translate your abstract dreams into tangible, actionable steps, providing a roadmap that keeps you focused and motivated. Setting **SMART goals—specific, measurable, achievable, relevant, and time-bound**—ensures your aspirations are grounded in reality and within reach. These goals should be revisited and refined regularly to stay aligned with your evolving vision and circumstances.

Taking deliberate actions is where the rubber meets the road. It is in the realm of action that visions are transformed from mere thoughts into reality. Every step you take, no matter how small, brings you closer to your envisioned future. This requires a combination of **strategic planning, resilience, and adaptability**. The journey is rarely linear; it is often fraught with obstacles and detours. However, through these challenges, you grow and develop the skills and attributes necessary to achieve your vision.

The techniques outlined in this chapter provide a comprehensive toolkit for anyone embarking on the journey of vision crafting. From self-reflection and visualization to goal setting and mentorship, these techniques offer practical and actionable steps to help you define and maintain a compelling vision. They are designed to be flexible and adaptable, allowing you to tailor them to your unique circumstances and aspirations. By integrating these techniques into your daily life, you create a structured yet dynamic process that supports your ongoing growth and development.

The **case studies of successful visionaries** presented in this chapter serves as a powerful illustration of the transformative power of a well-crafted vision. These individuals, through their unwavering commitment to their dreams, have achieved remarkable feats and left indelible marks on the world. Their journeys are testaments to the fact that with a clear vision, defined goals, and deliberate actions, it is possible to transcend the ordinary and achieve the extraordinary. They remind us that vision crafting is not just about personal success; it is about making a meaningful impact on the world and contributing to the greater good.

Embracing the art of vision crafting means committing to a lifelong journey of growth, learning, and transformation. It is about being open to new possibilities, staying curious, and continually pushing the boundaries of what is possible. It is about balancing ambition with contentment, and personal aspirations with a sense of responsibility towards others and the planet. By embracing this art, you become an active participant in the creation of your future, rather than a passive observer.

As you embark on this journey, remember that vision crafting is both an art and a science. It requires **creativity, intuition, and imagination**, as well as **discipline, strategy, and execution**. It is a holistic process that engages your mind, heart, and soul. By integrating all these elements, you can build a future that is not only successful but also fulfilling and meaningful.

Ultimately, vision crafting is about building your tomorrow with the actions you take today. It is about living with intention and purpose, guided by a vision that inspires and motivates you. By cherishing your visions, defining clear goals, and taking deliberate actions, you create a future that aligns with your deepest aspirations. You have the power to shape your destiny, to create a life that reflects your values and passions, and to make a lasting impact on the world.

2

Goal Setting Mastery

He who would have a life secure and blessed, a life freed from the miseries and failures to which so many fall victims, must carry the practice of the moral principles into every detail of his life, into every momentary duty and trivial transaction.

Setting goals is not merely a practical exercise; it is an ethical and philosophical endeavour that roots your life in purpose and direction. Goals act as the compass guiding you through life's complexities, ensuring that each step you take aligns with your deepest values and aspirations. This chapter delves into the intricate art of goal setting, providing you with the knowledge and tools to transform your dreams into tangible achievements.

The journey to a secure and blessed life is paved with disciplined goal setting. While dreams ignite the spark within us, goals provide the structured pathway to turn those dreams into reality. Understanding the difference between dreams and goals, employing the SMART goals framework, and distinguishing between long-term and short-term goals are essential components of mastering the art of goal setting.

Difference Between Dreams and Goals

Dreams and goals are often used interchangeably, but they represent distinct concepts. Understanding the difference between them is crucial for effective goal setting. They are the creative, often abstract visions that reside in the realm of our imagination. They are the compelling images and scenarios that motivate us and give us hope. Dreams are limitless and not bound by practical constraints; they serve as the initial inspiration and the driving force behind our ambitions. Goals, on the other hand, are concrete, actionable steps derived from our dreams. They are specific, measurable targets that guide our actions and decisions. Goals break down the vast expanse of dreams into manageable and achievable components.

Dreams: The Inspirational Spark

- **Characteristics of Dreams:**
  - *Abstract and Vague*: Dreams are often broad and lack specific details.
  - *Emotionally Driven:* They evoke strong emotions and a sense of excitement.
  - *Unconstrained by Reality*: Dreams are not limited by current circumstances or practical considerations.
  - *Nature of Dreams*: Dreams are the visions and aspirations that reside in our imagination. They are the ideal scenarios we wish to achieve in our lives, often characterised by their broad and abstract nature. Dreams inspire and motivate us, providing a sense of possibility and hope.
  - *Emotional Component*: Dreams evoke strong emotions and can be a source of joy, excitement, and motivation. They often reflect our deepest desires and passions.

- **Lack of Specificity:** Dreams lack the concrete details and specific steps required for realization. They are the "what" without the "how."

The Practical Blueprint

Characteristics of Goals:
1. **Specific and Detailed:** Goals are precise and clearly defined.
2. **Action-oriented:** They involve specific actions that need to be taken.
3. **Aligned with Reality:** Goals are realistic and consider current resources and constraints.
4. **Nature of Goals:** Goals are the actionable steps we take to turn our dreams into reality. They are specific, measurable, and time-bound objectives that guide our actions and decisions.
5. **Practical Component:** Goals are grounded in practicality. They break down dreams into achievable milestones, providing a clear roadmap for progress.
6. **Clarity and Focus:** Goals offer clarity and focus, outlining the specific steps needed to achieve the desired outcome. They transform the abstract nature of dreams into concrete plans.

SMART Goals Framework

The SMART goals framework is a powerful tool for setting effective goals. Let's explore each component in detail:

1. Specific

A specific goal clearly defines what you want to achieve. It answers the questions of who, what, where, when, and why. Goals should be clear and specific, answering the questions of Who, What, Where, When, Why, and How. Specificity helps focus efforts and clearly define what is to be accomplished.

1. **Example:** Instead of saying "I want to get fit," a specific goal would be "I want to lose 10 pounds in the next three months by exercising at the gym five times a week and following a healthy diet."
2. **Measurable**

A measurable goal includes criteria for tracking progress and determining when the goal is achieved. It quantifies the objective. Goals need to have criteria for measuring progress. This involves defining what success looks like and how progress will be tracked.

2. **Example:** "I want to save $5,000 in six months by setting aside $833.33 each month." "I want to increase my sales by 20% within the next six months by implementing a new marketing strategy."
3. **Achievable**

An achievable goal is realistic and attainable within your current capabilities and resources. It challenges you but is not impossible. Goals should be realistic and attainable, considering available resources and constraints. This involves setting goals that stretch your abilities but remain possible to achieve.

3. **Example:** "I want to read one book per month by dedicating 30 minutes to reading each day." "I want to save $5,000 this year by cutting unnecessary expenses and increasing my income through freelance work."
4. **Relevant**

A relevant goal aligns with your long-term objectives, values, and broader life aspirations. It is meaningful and significant. Goals should align with broader life objectives and be meaningful.

They need to be relevant to the direction you want your life or career to take.

- **Example:** "I want to enhance my professional skills by taking a course in project management, which will help me advance in my career." "I want to learn Spanish to enhance my career opportunities and prepare for a transfer to the company's office in Spain."
5. **Time-bound**

A time-bound goal has a specific deadline or timeframe for completion. It creates a sense of urgency and helps prioritise tasks. Every goal should have a deadline or a time frame for completion. This creates a sense of urgency and helps prioritise tasks.

1. **Example:** "I want to complete my project proposal by the end of this month." "I want to complete my professional certification within the next 12 months by dedicating 10 hours a week to studying."

Long-term vs. Short-term Goals

Setting goals is a fundamental aspect of personal and professional development. The distinction between long-term and short-term goals is crucial for creating a balanced and effective goal-setting strategy. Understanding these differences helps you to align your efforts and resources towards achieving your desired outcomes efficiently.

Long-term Goals

Long-term goals are objectives that you aim to achieve over an extended period, typically several years or even decades. These goals represent significant milestones in your life or career, requiring sustained effort and commitment.

Characteristics:

- ***Visionary***: Long-term goals are aligned with your broader vision and life purpose. They reflect your ultimate aspirations and desired outcomes, guiding your daily activities and decisions towards a larger objective.
- • ***Broad Scope***: These goals encompass various aspects of your life, including career, education, personal growth, relationships, and financial stability. They are not confined to a single area but span across different domains to create a holistic improvement in your life.
- • ***Incremental Progress***: Achieving long-term goals requires consistent effort and incremental progress over time. They are often broken down into smaller, manageable steps to make the journey towards them more feasible and less overwhelming.
- • ***Complex and Multifaceted***: Long-term goals usually involve multiple steps and require a coordinated effort across different areas of your life. They demand a strategic approach and a clear plan to navigate the complexities involved.
- • ***Impactful***: The achievement of long-term goals can have a substantial impact on your life. They often signify major accomplishments and can lead to significant personal and professional transformation.

Examples:

- **Career Advancement**: Aiming to become a senior executive in your organisation or starting your own successful business. This goal involves continuous learning, networking, gaining diverse experiences, and developing leadership skills over several years.
- **Education**: Aspiring to earn a graduate degree or professional

certification. This requires a long-term commitment to studying, attending classes, and completing various academic requirements.
- **Personal Growth**: Setting a goal to write a book or master a new language. These goals demand persistent effort, regular practice, and a passion for learning and self-improvement.
- **Financial Stability**: Planning to build a substantial retirement fund or purchasing a home. This involves disciplined saving, smart investment strategies, and financial planning over many years.

By understanding and embracing the nature of long-term goals, you can set a clear direction for your future, ensuring that your daily efforts contribute towards your ultimate life aspirations.

Short-term Goals

Short-term goals are the stepping stones that pave the way towards achieving your long-term aspirations. These are objectives that you aim to accomplish in the near future, typically within a few days, weeks, or months. By focusing on short-term goals, you can make immediate progress and maintain momentum towards your larger ambitions.

Characteristics:

1. **Immediate Focus**: Short-term goals provide immediate direction and focus. They help you prioritise your tasks and activities, ensuring that you stay on track and avoid distractions. By setting these goals, you can concentrate on what needs to be done right now to move closer to your ultimate objectives.
2. **Specificity**: One of the defining features of short-term goals is their high level of specificity. Unlike long-term goals, which

can be broad and visionary, short-term goals are detailed and actionable. They outline the exact steps you need to take, making it easier to plan and execute your tasks efficiently.
3. **Measurable Outcomes**: Short-term goals come with clear, measurable outcomes. This allows you to track your progress and evaluate your performance. By setting quantifiable targets, you can easily determine whether you are on the right path and make any necessary adjustments to stay aligned with your long-term goals.

Examples:
- **Daily Tasks**: These are the small, day-to-day activities that contribute to your overall productivity and success. Examples include completing a report, attending a meeting, or organising your workspace. These tasks may seem minor, but they play a crucial role in maintaining your daily efficiency and keeping you motivated.
- **Weekly Objectives**: These goals are slightly larger in scope and require consistent effort throughout the week. Examples include exercising five times a week, meal planning, or networking with industry professionals. By setting weekly objectives, you can establish a routine and create a sense of accomplishment as you complete each task.
- **Monthly Milestones**: These are more substantial goals that you aim to achieve within a month. Examples include learning a new skill, saving a specific amount of money, or achieving a sales target. Monthly milestones help you see tangible progress over a longer period and provide a sense of achievement that keeps you motivated for future goals.

The Importance of Short-term Goals:
- Short-term goals are essential for maintaining focus and

momentum. They break down the larger, long-term goals into manageable pieces, making it easier to stay motivated and on track. By setting and achieving short-term goals, you can build confidence and develop a habit of continuous improvement.
- Furthermore, short-term goals allow you to adapt and respond to changes quickly. If you encounter obstacles or setbacks, you can adjust your short-term goals accordingly without losing sight of your long-term vision. This flexibility ensures that you remain resilient and capable of navigating challenges as they arise.

In summary, short-term goals are a critical component of effective goal-setting. They provide immediate focus, specific actions, and measurable outcomes that drive you towards your long-term aspirations. By setting and achieving short-term goals, you can maintain momentum, build confidence, and make consistent progress in all areas of your life.

Integrating Long-term and Short-term Goals

For a balanced and effective goal-setting strategy, it is essential to integrate long-term and short-term goals. This integration ensures that your daily actions align with your broader vision, creating a cohesive and purposeful approach to personal and professional growth. By harmonizing these two types of goals, you can navigate the complexities of life with clarity and direction, ensuring that each step you take is a meaningful contribution towards your ultimate aspirations.

1. Alignment and Consistency

Ensure Alignment: The first step in integrating long-term and short-term goals is to ensure alignment between them. This requires regular reflection and assessment of your long-term goals to confirm that your short-term objectives are contributing towards them. It's essential to create a synergy where each short-term goal is a building block that supports the achievement of your long-term vision. For instance, if your long-term goal is to become a senior executive, your short-term goals might include completing relevant courses, networking with industry leaders, and gaining diverse work experiences. Regularly reviewing your goals will help you stay on course and make necessary adjustments to maintain alignment.

Maintain Consistency: Consistency is the linchpin of successful goal achievement. It's not enough to set short-term goals; you must also work on them consistently to build momentum and make steady progress towards your long-term objectives. Developing a routine that incorporates daily, weekly, and monthly actions aligned with your goals can help maintain this consistency. For example, setting aside specific times for professional development activities or regular check-ins to assess your progress ensures that you remain committed and motivated.

2. Breaking Down Long-term Goals

Divide into Milestones: Long-term goals can often seem daunting due to their scale and scope. To make them more manageable, it's crucial to break them down into smaller, achievable milestones. Each milestone represents a significant step towards your larger goal, making the overall objective less overwhelming and more attainable. For instance, if your long-term goal is to write a book, you could divide it into milestones such as completing an outline, writing each chapter, and revising the manuscript. This approach allows you to celebrate small victories along the way, keeping you motivated and focused.

Create Action Plans: Once you have identified the milestones, the next step is to develop detailed action plans for each one. These plans should outline the specific steps needed to achieve each milestone, providing a clear roadmap to follow. Action plans should include timelines, resources required, and any potential obstacles you might encounter. For example, if one of your milestones is to earn a professional certification, your action plan could detail the study schedule, registration process, and preparation for the examination. Having a well-structured plan helps maintain focus and direction, ensuring that you make consistent progress.

3. Regular Review and Adjustment

Regular Check-ins: To ensure that you stay on track, it is essential to schedule regular check-ins to review your progress on both short-term and long-term goals. These check-ins can be weekly, monthly, or quarterly, depending on your preference and the nature of your goals. During these sessions, assess what is working well and identify areas that may need improvement. Reflecting on your progress allows you to recognize your achievements and stay motivated, while also pinpointing any challenges that require attention.

Adapt and Adjust: Flexibility is crucial in the goal-setting process, as life is dynamic and circumstances can change unexpectedly. Be willing to adapt and adjust your goals and plans as needed. For example, if an unforeseen event impacts your ability to work on a particular short-term goal, reassess your priorities and adjust your timeline accordingly. This adaptability ensures that you remain resilient and capable of navigating any obstacles that come your way. Regularly updating your action plans based on these reflections helps you stay aligned with your long-term vision, even as you navigate changes and challenges. Integrating long-term and short-term goals into a cohesive strategy is essential for achieving sustained success and personal fulfilment. By ensuring alignment and consistency, breaking down long-term goals into manageable milestones, and regularly reviewing and adjusting your plans, you create a robust framework that supports your growth and development. This comprehensive approach not only keeps you focused on your ultimate aspirations but also allows you to adapt and thrive in the face of change, ensuring that each step you take is purposeful and aligned with your broader vision.

Practical Steps for Effective Goal Setting

1. **Identify Your Core Values**
   o **Understand Your Values:** Reflect on your core values and principles. Understanding what matters most to you will help you set meaningful and relevant goals.
   o **Align Goals with Values:** Ensure that your goals align with your core values. Goals that reflect your values are more likely to be fulfilling and motivating.
2. **Set Clear and Specific Goals**
   o **Define Specific Goals:** Clearly define your goals, specifying what you want to achieve and why it is important to you. Vague goals lead to vague outcomes.
   o **Use the SMART Framework:** Apply the SMART framework to make your goals Specific, Measurable, Achievable, Relevant, and Time-bound.
3. **Develop an Action Plan**
   o **Outline Steps:** Develop a detailed action plan for each goal, outlining the specific steps you need to take to achieve it. Break down larger tasks into smaller, manageable actions.
   o **Assign Deadlines:** Assign deadlines to each step in your action plan to create a sense of urgency and prioritise tasks.

4. **Monitor and Track Progress**
   o **Track Your Progress:** Regularly track your progress toward your goals. Use tools such as journals, spreadsheets, or goal-tracking apps to monitor your achievements.
   o **Celebrate Milestones:** Celebrate your achievements and milestones along the way. Recognizing your progress boosts motivation and reinforces positive behaviour.
5. **Stay Accountable**
   o **Find an Accountability Partner:** Share your goals with a trusted friend, mentor, or coach who can provide support and hold you accountable.
   o **Join a Group:** Consider joining a group or community with similar goals. The support and encouragement from like-minded individuals can be invaluable.
6. **Reflect and Reassess**
   o **Regular Reflection:** Schedule regular reflection sessions to review your goals and progress. Reflect on what is working and what needs improvement.
   o **Adjust as Needed:** Be open to adjusting your goals and plans based on your reflections. Flexibility allows you to stay aligned with your evolving values and circumstances.

Case Studies of Successful Goal Setting

1. **Jeff Bezos: Founder of Amazon**
   o **Vision:** Jeff Bezos envisioned creating an online marketplace that would offer a vast selection of products and prioritise customer satisfaction.
   o **SMART Goals:** Bezos set specific goals for expanding product categories, improving delivery times, and enhancing customer experience. Each goal was

measurable, achievable, relevant, and time-bound.
- **Outcome:** Amazon grew from a small online bookstore to one of the world's largest e-commerce platforms, revolutionizing retail and customer service.

2. **Serena Williams: Tennis Champion**
   - **Vision:** Serena Williams aimed to become one of the greatest tennis players of all time, breaking records and winning numerous Grand Slam titles.
   - **SMART Goals:** Williams set specific training goals, focusing on improving her serve, fitness, and mental resilience. She established measurable milestones for each tennis season.
   - **Outcome:** Williams achieved her vision, winning 23 Grand Slam singles titles and becoming an iconic figure in sports.

3. **Bill Gates: Co-founder of Microsoft**
   - **Vision:** Bill Gates envisioned a world where every household and business would have a personal computer.
   - **SMART Goals:** Gates set clear goals for software development, market penetration, and strategic partnerships. Each goal was specific, measurable, and aligned with his vision.
   - **Outcome:** Microsoft became a dominant force in the technology industry, transforming how people and businesses use computers.

4. **Malala Yousafzai: Education Advocate**
   - **Vision:** Malala Yousafzai aimed to ensure that girls worldwide have access to education, advocating for their rights and empowerment.
   - **SMART Goals:** Yousafzai set specific goals for raising awareness, influencing policy changes, and supporting educational programs. Her goals were measurable and

time-bound.
- o **Outcome:** Malala's advocacy work earned her the Nobel Peace Prize, and her efforts continue to impact millions of girls globally.

Goal setting is an essential practice for anyone aspiring to lead a life of purpose and achievement. It serves as a foundational pillar that guides your actions and decisions, ensuring that you remain focused and motivated towards your desired outcomes. By understanding the difference between dreams and goals, applying the SMART goals framework, and balancing long-term and short-term objectives, you can create a clear roadmap for success. Incorporating ethical principles into all facets of your goal-setting process guarantees that your endeavours are both effective and imbued with meaning and fulfilment.

Understanding the Difference Between Dreams and Goals

At the outset, it's crucial to differentiate between dreams and goals. Dreams are the visions and aspirations that inspire you, while goals are the actionable steps you take to turn those dreams into reality. Dreams provide the motivation and inspiration needed to strive for something greater, but without concrete goals, they remain intangible and elusive. Goals, on the other hand, are specific, measurable, achievable, relevant, and time-bound (SMART) objectives that bring structure and clarity to your ambitions. By translating your dreams into SMART goals, you create a tangible path towards achieving your aspirations.

Balancing Long-term and Short-term Objectives

A balanced approach to goal setting involves integrating both long-term and short-term objectives. Long-term goals provide the overarching vision and direction for your life, representing significant milestones that you aim to achieve over an extended period. These goals require sustained effort and commitment, and they often encompass various aspects of your personal and professional life.

Short-term goals, on the other hand, are the immediate steps that contribute to your long-term objectives. They provide focus and direction in the near term, ensuring that you make consistent progress towards your larger ambitions. By breaking down long-term goals into smaller, manageable milestones, you can maintain momentum and avoid feeling overwhelmed.

Integrating Ethical Principles into Goal Setting

Incorporating ethical principles into your goal-setting process is essential for ensuring that your pursuits are not only effective but also meaningful and fulfilling. Ethical goal setting involves considering the impact of your actions on others and striving to achieve your objectives in a way that aligns with your values and principles. This approach fosters a sense of integrity and purpose, making your achievements more rewarding.

Practical Steps and Case Studies

The practical steps and case studies provided in this chapter offer a comprehensive guide to mastering the art of goal setting. These real-life examples illustrate how individuals have successfully applied the principles and techniques discussed to achieve their dreams. By studying these cases, you can gain valuable insights and inspiration to apply to your own goal-setting journey.

Embrace and Transform

Embrace these techniques, and you will be well-equipped to transform your dreams into reality. Effective goal setting empowers you to take control of your life, making deliberate choices that lead to success and fulfilment. By defining clear, practical goals and working towards them, you can live a secure, blessed life without the sorrows and failures that so many suffer.

3

Time Management Techniques

> *Time management is the methodical process of organising and regulating how much time to allocate to various activities to maximize effectiveness, efficiency, and productivity.*

The athlete who prematurely crossed the finish line would never earn the victory. He must first stand at the starting line, attentive and ready, awaiting the signal to commence. Even then, securing a good start is crucial if he is to triumph. This analogy vividly illustrates the principles of time management.

Achieving mastery in time management is similar to an athlete gearing up for a significant race; it necessitates meticulous planning, unwavering precision, and steadfast discipline. Much like the athlete who needs to ensure a proper start to position himself for success, individuals must strategically manage their time to accomplish their objectives. Let's delve deeper into this analogy to understand the essence and importance of time management.

Preparation and Planning: The Foundation of Success

Before the race, an athlete undergoes rigorous training, creating a structured regimen that addresses all aspects of physical and mental conditioning. This preparatory phase is akin to the initial step in time management, where one must meticulously plan their schedule. Effective time management starts with a clear understanding of tasks and goals. It involves setting specific, measurable objectives and determining the most efficient path to achieve them. Without this foundational planning, efforts can become haphazard and unproductive.

Precision in Execution: The Art of Focus

During the race, an athlete's focus is laser-sharp, concentrating on each stride, each breath, ensuring that every movement is optimized for performance. Similarly, in time management, precision is vital. This means allocating appropriate amounts of time to each task based on its priority and complexity. It involves being aware of one's peak productivity periods and scheduling demanding tasks during these times. Just as an athlete tunes out distractions to maintain peak performance, individuals must learn to minimize interruptions and maintain focus to enhance productivity.

Discipline: The Sustaining Force

An athlete's success hinges on unwavering discipline – adhering to training schedules, maintaining dietary restrictions, and consistently pushing through physical and mental barriers. Discipline in time management translates to sticking to planned schedules, resisting the temptation to procrastinate, and persistently pursuing one's goals despite obstacles. It involves regular self-assessment and adjustment of strategies to ensure that time is being utilized effectively. This disciplined approach helps in developing a routine that optimizes performance.

The Importance of a Good Start

For an athlete, the start of the race sets the tone for the entire performance. A strong start can provide a competitive edge, while a poor start can be difficult to recover from. In time management, beginning the day with a clear plan and a positive mindset can significantly influence productivity levels. Establishing a morning routine that includes planning, setting priorities, and mental preparation can lead to a more organised and productive day. Just as athletes warm up to prepare their bodies, individuals can benefit from mental warm-ups such as meditation, reviewing goals, or even light physical exercise.

Continuous Improvement: The Path to Mastery

Athletes continuously seek to improve their performance, analysing each race to identify strengths and weaknesses, and making necessary adjustments to their training regimens. In time management, continuous improvement involves regularly reviewing how time is spent, identifying patterns of inefficiency, and implementing changes to enhance productivity. This might include adopting new tools and techniques, seeking feedback, and staying updated with best practices in time management. The goal is to create a dynamic and adaptive approach that evolves with changing demands and priorities.

Analogous Examples and Theoretical Insights

Consider the journey of a marathon runner preparing for a major competition. This athlete meticulously plans their training schedule, balancing long runs with strength training and rest days. They focus on their diet, sleep, and even mental strategies to overcome fatigue and maintain motivation. Throughout their preparation, they track progress, adjust plans based on performance data, and stay committed to their goal. This holistic approach mirrors effective time management, where planning, execution, and continuous improvement are intertwined to achieve success.

Theories such as the Eisenhower Matrix or the Pomodoro Technique provide frameworks to enhance time management practices. The Eisenhower Matrix helps in categorizing tasks based on urgency and importance, enabling individuals to prioritise effectively. The Pomodoro Technique promotes focused work sessions followed by short breaks, improving concentration and preventing burnout. These theoretical models serve as tools to refine the time management process, much like training methodologies for athletes.

The Race Analogy Extended: Beyond the Finish Line

The race does not end at the finish line for an athlete; it is followed by a recovery phase, reflection, and planning for future competitions. Similarly, time management is not confined to the completion of tasks. It involves reflecting on what was achieved, analysing what worked and what did not, and planning for the next set of objectives. This continuous cycle of planning, execution, and reflection ensures sustained growth and productivity.

In Final Thoughts, mastering time management is a comprehensive process that mirrors the journey of an athlete preparing for and competing in a race. It requires thorough preparation, precise execution, and unwavering discipline. By understanding and applying these principles, individuals can optimize their use of time, achieve their goals, and ultimately enhance their overall productivity and quality of life. Just as an athlete must start correctly to have a chance at winning the race, individuals must manage their time effectively to reach their desired outcomes.

Importance of Time Management

1. **Enhanced Productivity**
   - ***Optimizing Output***: Effective time management is crucial for maximizing productivity. By carefully planning and prioritising tasks, individuals can focus their efforts on activities that yield the highest impact. This strategic approach ensures that more is accomplished in less time, significantly boosting overall productivity.
   - ***Streamlined Efficiency***: Time management reduces inefficiencies by minimizing wasted time and resources. With a well-structured plan, individuals can complete tasks more quickly and effectively, allowing them to move on to subsequent activities without unnecessary delays. This efficiency not only improves individual performance but also enhances organisational productivity.
2. **Improved Quality of Work**
   - ***Concentrated Focus***: When individuals manage their time effectively, they can allocate sufficient attention to each task. This concentrated effort results in higher-quality work, as individuals can thoroughly engage with their responsibilities without feeling rushed or distracted.
   - ***Error Minimization***: Proper time management helps individuals avoid the last-minute rush to meet deadlines, which often leads to mistakes and subpar work. By allocating adequate time for each task, individuals can ensure accuracy and attention to detail, ultimately producing better results.
3. **Stress Reduction**
   - ***Managing Overwhelm***: Effective time management

involves breaking down large, overwhelming tasks into smaller, more manageable chunks. This approach reduces stress and anxiety by making complex projects seem more attainable and less daunting. Individuals can tackle one step at a time, maintaining a sense of control and calm.
- **Work-Life Balance:** A well-managed schedule allows individuals to allocate time for both work and personal activities. This balance ensures that personal time and relaxation are not sacrificed for work commitments, promoting overall well-being and reducing stress levels.

4. **Achievement of Goals**
   - ***Defining a Clear Path***: Time management provides a structured approach to achieving goals. By organising tasks and setting priorities, individuals can create a clear path to their objectives. This clarity helps in maintaining focus and direction, ensuring that every minute is used purposefully toward goal attainment.
   - ***Tracking Progress***: Effective time management enables individuals to monitor their progress toward goals. Regularly reviewing and adjusting plans ensures that they stay on track and make necessary modifications to meet their targets. This ongoing assessment fosters a sense of accomplishment and motivation.

5. **Increased Opportunities**
   - ***Adapting to Flexibility***: Efficient time management creates the flexibility needed to accommodate unexpected opportunities. With a well-organised schedule, individuals can adapt to new prospects without disrupting existing plans. This adaptability allows them to seize opportunities that can lead to personal and professional growth.

- ***Professional Growth***: Demonstrating strong time management skills can significantly enhance an individual's professional reputation. Being known for effective time management can lead to increased responsibilities, promotions, and career advancement. Employers value individuals who can manage their time well, as it reflects reliability and competence.

Deep Dive into the Benefits of Time Management

1. **Maximizing Productivity Through Structured Planning**
   - ***Detailed Task Breakdown***: Breaking tasks into detailed, actionable steps helps in managing time more effectively. By creating a clear roadmap, individuals can navigate their responsibilities with greater precision and avoid feeling overwhelmed.
   - ***Priority Setting with Advanced Techniques***: Techniques like the Eisenhower Matrix and ABC Method enable individuals to categorize and prioritise tasks based on urgency and importance. This strategic prioritisation ensures that critical tasks receive the attention they deserve, while less important activities are scheduled appropriately.
2. **Enhancing Quality of Work Through Focused Effort**
   - ***Dedicated Work Sessions***: Allocating uninterrupted blocks of time for specific tasks allows for deeper concentration and higher quality outcomes. Techniques like time blocking and the Pomodoro Technique can help individuals maintain focus and productivity.
   - ***Quality Assurance Processes***: Implementing regular quality checks and reviews within the time management framework ensures that work meets high standards. These processes help in identifying and correcting errors

before final submission.
3. **Mitigating Stress and Promoting Balance**
    - *Implementing Relaxation Techniques:* Integrating relaxation and mindfulness practices into daily routines can significantly reduce stress. Techniques such as meditation, deep breathing exercises, and short breaks can help individuals maintain mental clarity and resilience.
    - *Creating Personal Time Buffers:* Scheduling dedicated personal time for hobbies, exercise, and relaxation ensures that individuals maintain a healthy work-life balance. These buffers prevent burnout and promote overall well-being.
4. **Leveraging Opportunities for Growth**
    - *Embracing Continuous Learning:* Allocating time for continuous learning and skill development can open new opportunities for career advancement. Engaging in professional development activities, such as attending workshops and pursuing certifications, enhances competencies and marketability.
    - *Networking and Relationship Building:* Effective time management allows individuals to allocate time for networking and building professional relationships. These connections can lead to new opportunities, collaborations, and career growth.

The significance of time management cannot be overstated. It serves as the cornerstone for enhanced productivity, improved quality of work, stress reduction, goal achievement, and increased opportunities. By adopting a structured approach to managing time, individuals can unlock their full potential and achieve success in both personal and professional realms. The key lies in understanding the importance of time management, implementing effective strategies, and continuously refining these practices to adapt to changing demands. Through diligent time management, individuals can create a balanced, productive, and fulfilling life, paving the way for lasting achievements and growth.

Effective Time Management Strategies

1. Prioritisation

Task Prioritisation Techniques

The Eisenhower Decision Matrix: A powerful tool for categorizing tasks based on urgency and importance, facilitating effective decision-making:

- **Urgent and Important**: These tasks require immediate attention and are critical for achieving key objectives. They should be tackled first to prevent crises and ensure high-priority goals are met.
- **Not Urgent but Important**: These tasks are essential but can be scheduled for later. They often relate to long-term goals and personal development, such as planning, relationship-building, and skill enhancement.
- **Urgent but Not Important**: These tasks demand quick action but do not significantly impact long-term goals. They can often be delegated to others to free up time for more critical activities.
- **Not Urgent and Not Important**: These tasks are neither time-sensitive nor impactful and can often be eliminated or minimized to avoid wasting time.

ABC Method: Another effective prioritisation technique that categorizes tasks into three groups:

- **A Tasks**: These are the most critical tasks that have the highest impact on achieving goals. They should be given top priority and completed first.
- **B Tasks**: Important tasks that are necessary but not as crucial as A tasks. They should be addressed after completing A tasks.
- **C Tasks**: These tasks are least important and should only be completed if time permits after A and B tasks.

2. Goal Setting

Defining Clear and Achievable Goals

- **Daily, Weekly, and Monthly Goals**: Breaking down long-term objectives into smaller, actionable tasks helps maintain focus and momentum. Daily goals keep you on track for immediate tasks, weekly goals ensure progress toward larger projects, and monthly goals align with long-term ambitions.

3. Planning and Scheduling

Organising Daily Activities

- **Daily Planners and To-Do Lists**: Utilizing planners to outline daily tasks and prioritise them helps in keeping track of responsibilities. To-do lists are essential tools for ensuring that nothing is forgotten and that all tasks are addressed systematically.
- **Time Blocking**: This technique involves allocating specific blocks of time for different activities, ensuring focused work periods and reducing distractions. By setting aside dedicated time for each task, productivity is maximized, and interruptions are minimized.
- **Buffer Time**: Including buffer times between tasks accounts for unexpected delays and prevents schedule overlaps. This

flexibility ensures that minor disruptions do not derail the entire day's plan.

4. Delegation

Optimizing Resource Allocation

- **Identify Delegable Tasks**: Determine which tasks can be delegated to others, freeing up your time for more critical activities. Delegating routine or less important tasks allows you to focus on high-impact work.
- **Trust and Empower**: Trust team members to handle delegated tasks efficiently and provide them with the necessary resources and support. Empowering others not only enhances productivity but also builds team morale and capability.

5. Avoiding Procrastination

- **Strategies to Combat Procrastination**
  - **Break Tasks into Smaller Steps**: Large tasks can be overwhelming and lead to procrastination. By breaking them into smaller, manageable steps, tasks become less daunting and more achievable.
  - **Set Personal Deadlines**: Even for tasks without strict deadlines, setting personal deadlines creates a sense of urgency and motivates timely completion.
  - **Eliminate Distractions**: Identify and eliminate distractions that contribute to procrastination, such as social media, unnecessary meetings, and clutter. Creating a focused work environment helps maintain productivity.

6. Time Management Techniques
- **Implementing Proven Techniques**
  - **Pomodoro Technique**: Work for 25 minutes, then take a 5-minute break. After four cycles, take a longer break. This technique boosts focus and productivity by encouraging short, intense work periods followed by rest.
  - **Pareto Principle (80/20 Rule)**: Focus on the 20% of tasks that yield 80% of the results. Prioritising high-impact activities maximizes efficiency and ensures that efforts are directed toward the most productive tasks.
  - **Getting Things Done (GTD)**: Capture all tasks and ideas, clarify actions, organise tasks by category, review regularly, and engage in productive work. This comprehensive approach ensures that nothing is overlooked and that tasks are systematically addressed.

7. Continuous Improvement
- **Enhancing Time Management Practices**
  - **Reflect and Review**: Regularly review your time management strategies and their effectiveness. Reflect on what works and what needs adjustment, allowing for continuous improvement and adaptation to changing circumstances.
  - **Seek Feedback**: Get feedback from peers and mentors on your time management practices and be open to suggestions for improvement. Constructive feedback provides valuable insights and helps refine your approach for better results.

Expanding Each Strategy with Detailed Examples and Insights

1. Advanced Prioritisation Techniques

Applying the Eisenhower Matrix to Real-Life Scenarios

Imagine a busy project manager juggling multiple responsibilities. By categorizing tasks using the Eisenhower Matrix, they can identify that client meetings and urgent project deadlines fall under 'Urgent and Important,' strategic planning for future projects falls under 'Not Urgent but Important,' routine administrative tasks fall under 'Urgent but Not Important,' and non-essential social media browsing falls under 'Not Urgent and Not Important.' This clear categorization allows the project manager to focus on what truly matters and delegate or eliminate less critical tasks.

Refining the ABC Method for Personal and Professional Tasks

A software developer can use the ABC Method to prioritise their daily tasks. 'A' tasks might include completing a critical feature for a software release, 'B' tasks could involve attending team meetings and reviewing code, and 'C' tasks might consist of updating documentation or responding to non-urgent emails. By systematically addressing 'A' tasks first, the developer ensures that the most impactful work is completed.

2. Comprehensive Goal Setting Approaches

Developing a Multi-Tiered Goal System

An entrepreneur might set long-term goals, such as launching a new product within a year. This long-term goal is broken down into monthly milestones, such as product design, prototype development, and market testing. Each monthly milestone is further divided into weekly objectives and daily tasks. This tiered approach ensures that every action taken contributes to the overarching goal, keeping the entrepreneur focused and motivated.

Utilizing SMART Goals in Various Contexts

A fitness enthusiast aiming to improve their health might set a SMART goal to "Lose 10 pounds in 3 months by exercising for 30 minutes daily and reducing calorie intake by 500 calories per day." This goal is Specific (lose 10 pounds), Measurable (weigh-ins), Achievable (realistic weight loss), Relevant (improving health), and Time-bound (3 months).

3. Advanced Planning and Scheduling Techniques

Integrating Daily Planners with Digital Tools

A marketing professional might use a combination of a physical planner and digital tools like Trello or Asana. The physical planner provides a tangible way to outline daily tasks, while the digital tools offer advanced features like task dependencies, deadlines, and team collaboration. This hybrid approach maximizes organisation and productivity.

Enhancing Time Blocking with Detailed Scheduling

A writer could allocate specific blocks of time for different activities, such as research, writing, editing, and breaks. By creating a detailed schedule with precise time blocks, the writer ensures focused work periods and minimizes distractions. For example, mornings could be dedicated to writing when energy levels are high, afternoons to research, and evenings to editing and review.

4. Effective Delegation Practices

Delegation in a Team Environment

A team leader in a corporate setting might identify tasks that can be delegated to team members, such as data analysis, report generation, or routine client communications. By trusting and empowering team members to handle these tasks, the leader can focus on strategic planning and high-level decision-making, enhancing overall team productivity.

Empowering Team Members through Training and Support

A project manager might delegate a complex task to a junior team member, providing them with the necessary training and resources. This not only frees up the manager's time but also helps in skill development and confidence-building for the junior member, fostering a more capable and resilient team.

1. Proactive Approaches to Avoiding Procrastination

Breaking Down Complex Projects with Detailed Planning

A student working on a thesis might feel overwhelmed by the sheer volume of work. By breaking the project into smaller steps, such as literature review, data collection, analysis, and writing chapters, the student can tackle each part individually, making the overall task more manageable.

Setting Incremental Deadlines for Continuous Progress

A freelancer might set personal deadlines for each stage of a project, such as completing the first draft in two weeks, revising in one week, and finalizing within another week. These incremental deadlines create a sense of urgency and ensure continuous progress, preventing procrastination.

Creating a Distraction-Free Work Environment

An architect might design a distraction-free workspace by eliminating unnecessary items, turning off notifications, and setting specific times for checking emails and messages. This focused environment enhances concentration and reduces the likelihood of procrastination.

6. Implementing Advanced Time Management Techniques

Using the Pomodoro Technique for Enhanced Focus

A software engineer might implement the Pomodoro Technique by working in 25-minute intervals with short breaks. After four intervals, a longer break is taken. This structured approach helps maintain high levels of focus and productivity, especially during coding and debugging sessions.

Applying the Pareto Principle for Maximum Impact

A sales manager might identify that 20% of clients generate 80% of revenue. By focusing efforts on these high-value clients, the manager can maximize sales performance and ensure that time and resources are directed toward the most impactful activities.

Adopting the Getting Things Done (GTD) Methodology

A content creator might use the GTD methodology to capture all ideas and tasks in a trusted system, clarify the next actions for each task, organise tasks by category (such as content creation, editing, and promotion), review regularly, and engage in productive work. This comprehensive approach ensures that all tasks are managed systematically and nothing is overlooked.

7. Continuous Improvement through Reflection and Feedback

Regular Self-Assessment and Adaptation

A financial analyst might set aside time each week to review their time management practices. By reflecting on what strategies worked well and identifying areas for improvement, the analyst can continuously adapt their approach to enhance productivity.

Seeking Constructive Feedback from Peers

A team leader might solicit feedback from team members on their time management practices. This feedback provides valuable insights and helps the leader identify blind spots or areas for improvement, leading to more effective time management and better team collaboration.

Effective time management requires prioritisation, goal setting, planning, delegating, procrastination avoidance, and ongoing development. By using and developing these tactics, people can maximise time, productivity, and success. Time management boosts productivity, reduces stress, and improves balance and fulfilment in personal and professional life. If you follow these tips and keep improving, you can manage your time and succeed.

Practical Applications of Time Management

6. Balancing Work and Personal Life

Work-Life Integration

Strive for a harmonious integration of work and personal life by setting boundaries and Prioritising tasks that align with your values.

Dedicated Personal Time

Schedule dedicated time for personal activities, hobbies, and relaxation to maintain a healthy work-life balance.

7. Managing Meetings and Communication

Effective Meetings

Schedule meetings with clear agendas, objectives, and time limits to ensure productive and focused discussions.

Communication Tools

Use communication tools like Slack or Microsoft Teams to streamline team communication and reduce the need for excessive meetings.

8. Handling Interruptions and Emergencies

Plan for Interruptions

Anticipate potential interruptions and plan buffer times in your schedule to accommodate unexpected events.

Emergency Protocols

Establish protocols for handling emergencies efficiently without derailing your entire schedule.

9. Developing a Routine

Consistent Routine

Establish a consistent daily routine that includes work, exercise, meals, and relaxation to create a sense of structure and predictability.

Morning and Evening Rituals

Develop morning and evening rituals to start and end your day with intention and focus.

Theories and Examples

1. Theories of Time Management

- **Theory of Constraints (TOC):** This theory, developed by Eliyahu M. Goldratt, posits that every system has a bottleneck that limits its overall performance. In time management, identifying and addressing these bottlenecks can significantly improve efficiency and productivity.
- **Parkinson's Law:** This adage states that "work expands to fill the time available for its completion." Understanding this concept helps individuals set realistic deadlines to avoid unnecessary time consumption.
- **Hawthorne Effect:** Named after a series of studies conducted at the Hawthorne Works, this effect suggests that individuals improve their performance when they are aware they are being observed. Time tracking and accountability measures can harness this effect to enhance productivity.

2. Real-Life Examples

- **Steve Jobs:** Known for his meticulous time management, Jobs would prioritise his work by focusing on a few critical tasks that had the most significant impact on his company's success. His ability to eliminate distractions and stay focused on his vision was a key factor in Apple's innovation.
- **Elon Musk:** Musk is famous for his rigorous time-blocking method, where he schedules his day in five-minute increments. This level of detailed planning allows him to

juggle multiple high-stakes ventures like Tesla and SpaceX efficiently.
- **Benjamin Franklin**: An early advocate of time management, Franklin followed a strict daily schedule that included time for work, study, and personal reflection. His practice of setting specific goals and reviewing his progress daily was instrumental in his many accomplishments.

Mastering time management is essential for achieving personal and professional success. By understanding the importance of time management, implementing effective strategies, and utilizing the right tools and apps, you can enhance productivity, reduce stress, and achieve your goals. Remember, just like an athlete who begins by facing the starter and toeing the mark, a good start in time management sets the foundation for winning the race. Embrace these techniques and tools, and you will be well-equipped to manage your time effectively, leading to a more secure and blessed life.

PART ONE

THE MINDSET FOR SUCCESS

4

Developing a Growth Mindset

Dreamers stand as the true saviours of our world.

Just as the visible world is underpinned by the invisible forces, humanity, through all its struggles, errors, and mundane tasks, is continuously sustained and inspired by the beautiful visions of solitary dreamers. These individuals, who possess the extraordinary ability to imagine realities beyond the current limitations, are the torchbearers of innovation and advancement. Their dreams, conceived in solitude, offer nourishment and hope to humanity amidst trials and adversities.

Understanding the Growth Mindset

The notion of a growth mindset is anchored in the profound belief that our talents and intelligence are not static traits but dynamic qualities that can be cultivated through dedication, hard work, and the right attitude. This concept revolutionizes the way we perceive our potential, suggesting that with persistence and a positive mindset, we can continually develop and improve our capabilities.

The Role of Dreamers in Shaping the Future

Dreamers, those visionary individuals who can see beyond the constraints of the present, play a crucial role in driving progress and innovation. Their ability to envision a better future and work towards it, even in isolation, has been a cornerstone of human advancement. Their solitary dreams, fueled by hope and imagination, become the foundation upon which new ideas and solutions are built.

Inspiration Through Solitude

The process of dreaming and envisioning often takes place in solitude, where distractions are minimal, and the mind can explore uncharted territories. It is in these moments of quiet reflection that dreamers formulate ideas that challenge the status quo and propose new ways of thinking and doing. These visions, though born in solitude, have the power to inspire and uplift entire communities and societies.

The Transformative Power of a Growth Mindset

Cultivating a growth mindset transforms the way we approach life's challenges. By believing that our abilities can be developed, we become more resilient in the face of adversity. This mindset encourages us to embrace challenges, persist through setbacks, and see effort as a pathway to mastery. It fosters a love for learning and a desire to continuously improve, which are essential traits for personal and professional success.

Nurturing Resilience and Adaptability

A growth mindset equips individuals with the resilience needed to navigate the inevitable difficulties of life. By viewing failures as opportunities for learning rather than as reflections of our abilities, we become more adaptable and open to change. This adaptability is crucial in a world that is constantly evolving and presenting new challenges.

Becoming More Resilient and Successful

Understanding and adopting a growth mindset can fundamentally change our approach to life. It makes us more resilient, as we no longer see failures as insurmountable obstacles but as stepping stones to success. This shift in perspective allows us to tackle challenges with greater confidence and determination, ultimately leading to higher levels of achievement and fulfilment.

The Invisible Sustenance of Vision

The concept that the visible world is sustained by the invisible highlights the importance of inner vision and belief. Dreamers, with their internal visions and aspirations, provide a form of invisible sustenance to humanity. Their dreams, though intangible, have very real impacts on the world, driving progress and fostering hope.

Challenges as Catalysts for Growth

Challenges and adversities, often seen as negative experiences, are reinterpreted through the lens of a growth mindset. These difficulties become catalysts for growth and development. Dreamers, with their visionary outlook, use these challenges to fuel their creativity and innovation, turning obstacles into opportunities for advancement.

The Solitary Dreamer's Journey

The journey of a dreamer is often a solitary one, marked by moments of introspection and quiet contemplation. However, this solitude is not a hindrance but a vital part of the creative process. It allows dreamers to connect deeply with their inner thoughts and aspirations, leading to the development of ideas that can transform the world.

The Power of Dedication and Hard Work

The belief in the ability to grow and develop through dedication and hard work is at the core of the growth mindset. This belief drives individuals to put in the necessary effort to achieve their goals. It underscores the importance of persistence and discipline, qualities that are essential for realizing one's dreams and making significant contributions to society.

Envisioning Beyond Current Realities

Dreamers have the unique ability to envision possibilities that lie beyond the current reality. This forward-thinking perspective is crucial for innovation and progress. By imagining what could be, rather than being constrained by what is, dreamers pave the way for new advancements and breakthroughs.

Inspiring Humanity Through Vision

The visions of dreamers, though often conceived in isolation, have a profound impact on humanity. They provide inspiration and guidance, helping people navigate through their own challenges. These visionary ideas serve as beacons of hope, reminding us of our potential to overcome difficulties and achieve greatness.

The Impact of Solitary Dreams on Collective Progress

While the process of dreaming is often a solitary one, its effects are far-reaching. The ideas and innovations that emerge from the minds of solitary dreamers can lead to collective progress and improvement. By sharing their visions with the world, dreamers contribute to the collective advancement of society.

Cultivating a Growth Mindset for Personal and Professional Success

Adopting a growth mindset can lead to significant improvements in both personal and professional spheres. It encourages continuous learning and development, which are key to achieving long-term success. By fostering a positive attitude towards challenges and setbacks, individuals can enhance their resilience and adaptability, making them better equipped to handle the demands of a rapidly changing world.

Final Thoughts: Embrace the Dreamer Within

The journey of developing a growth mindset is one of continuous effort and dedication. By understanding the principles of a growth mindset and applying them to our lives, we can unlock our full potential and achieve remarkable growth and transformation. Just as the dreamers who envision possibilities beyond the present have sustained and inspired humanity, we too can become visionaries who drive progress and innovation. With the right mindset, dedication, and hard work, we can make a lasting impact on ourselves and the world around us. Embrace the dreamer within and embark on a journey of growth and discovery.

Fixed Mindset vs. Growth Mindset

1. Fixed Mindset

- A fixed mindset refers to the belief that an individual's abilities and intelligence are unchangeable traits. People who subscribe to this mindset often think that talent is something one is born with, and there is little they can do to alter their inherent abilities.

- **Characteristics**:
  - **Fear of Failure**: Those with a fixed mindset tend to avoid challenges because they fear that failing will expose their perceived inadequacies. They view failure as a definitive indicator of their lack of inherent ability.
  - **Avoidance of Effort**: Effort is often seen as pointless by individuals with a fixed mindset. They believe that if something doesn't come naturally, it means they aren't capable of achieving it, leading them to shy away from putting in the necessary effort to improve.
  - **Response to Criticism**: Constructive criticism is often perceived as a personal attack by those with a fixed mindset. Instead of seeing feedback as a chance to grow, they interpret it as an affront to their abilities and often dismiss it.
  - **Perception of Others' Success**: The success of others can be threatening to individuals with a fixed mindset. They often see it as a comparison that highlights their own shortcomings, leading to feelings of envy and inadequacy.

2. Growth Mindset

- A growth mindset is the belief that abilities and intelligence can be developed through dedication, hard work, and perseverance. This mindset embraces the idea that everyone can grow and improve with consistent effort and the right strategies.
- **Characteristics**:
  - **Embrace of Challenges**: Individuals with a growth mindset view challenges as opportunities to learn and grow. They are willing to step out of their comfort zones and tackle difficult tasks because they believe that effort

leads to improvement.
- **Persistence**: In the face of setbacks, those with a growth mindset are more likely to persevere. They understand that effort is a crucial component of mastery and that obstacles are a natural part of the learning process.
- **Response to Criticism**: Feedback is welcomed and valued by individuals with a growth mindset. They see criticism as a tool for development and an opportunity to gain insights that can help them improve.
- **Perception of Others' Success**: Rather than feeling threatened, individuals with a growth mindset find inspiration in the success of others. They use it as motivation to work harder and enhance their own abilities, viewing others' achievements as proof that progress is possible.

In-Depth Analysis and Implications of Fixed and Growth Mindsets

1. Fixed Mindset: A Barrier to Personal Development

- *Static Perception of Abilities*: Those with a fixed mindset often believe that their talents and intelligence are static. This belief can create a self-fulfilling prophecy, where individuals limit their efforts and opportunities for growth, reinforcing the idea that they cannot improve.
- *Risk Aversion:* The fear of failure often leads to risk aversion. People with a fixed mindset may avoid new and challenging tasks, preferring to stick to what they know they can do well. This avoidance behaviour stifles personal development and learning.
- *Impact on Relationships:* The inability to accept constructive criticism can strain personal and professional relationships.

Individuals may become defensive and less open to feedback, which can hinder collaborative efforts and personal growth.

2. Growth Mindset: The Pathway to Continuous Improvement

- ***Dynamic Perception of Abilities***: Believing that abilities can be developed fosters a proactive approach to learning and self-improvement. Individuals with a growth mindset are more likely to engage in activities that challenge them and help them grow.
- ***Resilience and Adaptability***: Embracing challenges and persisting through setbacks builds resilience. These individuals are better equipped to adapt to changing circumstances and recover from failures, viewing them as temporary and surmountable.
- ***Enhanced Learning and Innovation:*** A growth mindset encourages continuous learning and creativity. By seeking out feedback and learning from mistakes, individuals can innovate and improve their performance over time.
- ***Positive Influence on Relationships:*** Openness to feedback and a focus on growth can lead to healthier, more constructive relationships. Individuals with a growth mindset are often more supportive and encouraging, fostering a collaborative and growth-oriented environment.

3. Practical Applications of Mindsets in Various Domains

- ***In Education:*** Educators who promote a growth mindset can significantly impact student learning. Encouraging students to view challenges as opportunities and praising effort rather than inherent ability can foster a love for learning and resilience in the face of academic difficulties.
- ***In the Workplace***: Organisations that cultivate a growth mindset culture can drive innovation and employee

development. Leaders who model a growth mindset by embracing challenges and seeking feedback can inspire their teams to strive for continuous improvement.
- ***In Personal Development:*** Applying a growth mindset to personal goals, such as health, fitness, and hobbies, can lead to significant improvements. Individuals who believe in their ability to grow are more likely to set ambitious goals and persist in achieving them despite setbacks.

4. Strategies for Cultivating a Growth Mindset

- ***Embracing Learning Opportunities:*** Actively seeking out new experiences and challenges that stretch one's abilities is crucial. This might involve taking on new projects, learning new skills, or stepping into unfamiliar roles that promote growth.
- ***Developing a Resilient Attitude:*** Building resilience involves changing the narrative around failure and setbacks. Viewing these experiences as valuable lessons rather than insurmountable obstacles helps in developing a growth-oriented mindset.
- ***Fostering a Positive Feedback Culture***: Surrounding oneself with supportive and constructive feedback environments can enhance growth. Engaging with mentors, peers, and colleagues who provide valuable insights can accelerate personal and professional development.
- ***Setting Incremental Goals:*** Breaking down long-term goals into smaller, manageable steps helps in maintaining motivation and focus. Celebrating small victories along the way reinforces the belief in one's ability to grow and succeed.

The Transformative Power of Mindsets

Understanding the difference between a fixed and growth mindset is the first step towards fostering personal and professional growth. By adopting a growth mindset, individuals can unlock their potential, embrace challenges, and transform setbacks into opportunities for learning. This mindset not only enhances individual performance but also promotes a culture of continuous improvement and collaboration. Embracing a growth mindset can lead to a more fulfilling, resilient, and successful life, paving the way for innovation and progress both personally and collectively.

Benefits of a Growth Mindset

1. Increased Resilience

- ***Handling Setbacks with Grace:*** A growth mindset transforms the perception of failure from a definitive end to a temporary setback. This change in perspective allows individuals to see failures as valuable learning experiences. Rather than being discouraged by failures, they are motivated to analyse what went wrong and make improvements, thereby fostering a resilient attitude.
- ***Embracing Change:*** A growth mindset promotes adaptability, making it easier for individuals to navigate the uncertainties and changes in life. By viewing challenges as opportunities to grow rather than threats, individuals maintain a positive outlook, which helps them adjust to new circumstances with ease.

2. Enhanced Learning and Development

- ***Commitment to Lifelong Learning:*** Individuals with a growth mindset are driven by an intrinsic love for learning. They are more inclined to pursue continuous education and skill enhancement. This commitment to lifelong learning keeps them intellectually curious and open to new ideas,

fostering ongoing personal and professional development.
- ***Advanced Problem-Solving Abilities:*** A growth mindset nurtures a sense of curiosity and innovative thinking. Challenges are approached as puzzles to be solved rather than insurmountable obstacles. This mindset encourages creative problem-solving, enabling individuals to develop effective solutions to complex issues.

3. Improved Performance

- ***Success in Academic and Professional Arenas:*** Research indicates that students and professionals with a growth mindset achieve higher levels of success. They are more likely to invest effort and persist through difficulties, which leads to better academic and professional outcomes. Their willingness to embrace challenges and learn from setbacks contributes significantly to their performance.
- ***Achieving Lofty Goals:*** A growth mindset drives individuals to set and pursue higher goals. The belief in their potential for improvement motivates them to strive for excellence and continuously raise their standards. This ambition results in achieving significant milestones and accomplishing long-term objectives.

4. Better Relationships

- ***Receptiveness to Feedback:*** People with a growth mindset are more open to receiving constructive feedback. They view feedback as a tool for growth rather than criticism, which helps improve both personal and professional relationships. This openness fosters better communication and understanding in interactions.
- ***Cultivating Empathy and Support:*** Individuals with a growth mindset are more likely to support and encourage

others. They understand the value of growth and learning, which translates into fostering a positive and collaborative environment. Their empathy and willingness to help others grow enhance the quality of their relationships.

5. Greater Happiness and Well-being

- ***Optimistic Life Perspective***: A growth mindset contributes to a more positive and optimistic outlook on life. By focusing on growth and improvement, individuals find greater satisfaction and happiness. This positive attitude helps them navigate life's challenges with confidence and hope.
- ***Stress Reduction:*** Focusing on effort and progress rather than perfection helps reduce stress. A growth mindset encourages individuals to appreciate the journey and the small steps of improvement, which alleviates the pressure to be perfect and diminishes stress levels.

In-Depth Exploration of Growth Mindset Benefits

1. Building Robust Resilience

- ***Transformative View of Failures:*** Embracing a growth mindset means recognizing that failure is not a permanent mark of inadequacy but a temporary hurdle that offers valuable insights. This perspective encourages individuals to experiment, take risks, and learn from their experiences, which builds a robust form of resilience.
- ***Thriving Amidst Change:*** Adaptability is a key benefit of a growth mindset. By anticipating and embracing change as a constant in life, individuals learn to thrive in dynamic environments. This ability to adapt quickly and efficiently to new situations is crucial in both personal and professional settings.

2. Lifelong Learning and Cognitive Growth

- *Continuous Intellectual Engagement:* Those with a growth mindset are perpetually engaged in learning. They seek out new knowledge, skills, and experiences that contribute to their cognitive growth. This ongoing pursuit of learning keeps their minds sharp and responsive to new challenges.
- *Innovative Approach to Problems:* Viewing challenges as opportunities to innovate fosters an environment where problem-solving becomes a creative endeavour. Individuals are more likely to explore unconventional solutions and think outside the box, leading to innovative breakthroughs.

3. Achieving Peak Performance

- *Enhanced Academic and Career Trajectories:* The determination and persistence characteristic of a growth mindset lead to improved academic and career trajectories. Students excel by overcoming academic challenges, while professionals advance by tackling complex projects and continuously enhancing their skills.
- *Setting and Reaching Ambitious Goals:* The drive to achieve higher goals is a hallmark of a growth mindset. Individuals are motivated to set ambitious targets and pursue them with vigor, which leads to remarkable achievements and sustained success.

4. Strengthening Interpersonal Connections

- *Effective Use of Feedback:* Constructive feedback becomes a catalyst for improvement rather than a source of discouragement. This attitude fosters open communication and trust in relationships, as individuals are more willing to listen, learn, and grow together.

- **Fostering Collaborative Environments:** A supportive and empathetic approach nurtures collaborative environments. Individuals with a growth mindset create spaces where others feel encouraged to share ideas, collaborate on projects, and support each other's growth.

5. Enhancing Overall Well-being

- **Positive and Hopeful Attitude:** By focusing on personal growth and continuous improvement, individuals cultivate a hopeful and positive attitude towards life. This mindset helps them appreciate the journey and find joy in the process, leading to a more fulfilling life.
- **Managing Stress through Progress:** Stress management is significantly improved when individuals focus on incremental progress rather than the end goal. Celebrating small victories and recognizing ongoing efforts help alleviate the pressure of perfectionism, resulting in reduced stress levels and better mental health.

The Holistic Impact of a Growth Mindset

Embracing a growth mindset offers profound benefits that permeate every aspect of life. From increased resilience and enhanced learning to improved performance and better relationships, the advantages are vast and transformative. By committing to this mindset, individuals can unlock their potential, achieve their goals, and experience greater happiness and well-being. This journey of continuous growth and self-improvement not only enriches personal and professional lives but also contributes to a more innovative and collaborative world.

Steps to Cultivate a Growth Mindset

1. **Acknowledge and Embrace Imperfection**

   o *Accepting Flaws:* Understand that imperfection is a natural part of the human experience. Embracing your flaws and mistakes is the first step towards growth.

   o *Learning from Mistakes:* View mistakes as valuable learning opportunities. Analyse what went wrong, what you can learn from it, and how you can improve.

2. **Challenge Yourself Regularly**

   o *Stepping Out of Comfort Zone:* Regularly push yourself out of your comfort zone. Take on new challenges and strive to improve in areas that you find difficult.

   o *Setting Stretch Goals:* Set goals that stretch your abilities and require effort and perseverance to achieve. This helps in building resilience and a growth-oriented mindset.

3. **Cultivate a Love for Learning**

   o *Pursue New Knowledge:* Continuously seek new knowledge and skills. Read books, take courses, and engage in activities that promote learning and personal growth.

   o *Curiosity:* Foster a sense of curiosity about the world. Ask questions, explore new ideas, and remain open to learning from various sources.

4. **Focus on Effort Over Outcome**

   o *Value the Process:* Shift your focus from the outcome to the process. Recognize and celebrate the effort you put into your tasks and learning experiences.

- **Incremental Progress:** Appreciate incremental progress and small wins. These build momentum and reinforce the growth mindset.

5. **Use the Power of "Yet"**

   - **Reframe Challenges:** Instead of saying, "I can't do this," say, "I can't do this yet." This simple shift in language reinforces the belief that ability can be developed over time.
   - **Positive Self-Talk:** Replace negative self-talk with growth-oriented affirmations. Encourage yourself by recognizing your potential for growth.

6. **Seek Constructive Feedback**

   - **Embrace Criticism:** Actively seek feedback from others and view it as a tool for improvement rather than a judgement on your abilities.
   - **Reflect on Feedback:** Reflect on the feedback you receive and use it to make actionable changes. This helps in continuous improvement and personal growth.

7. **Surround Yourself with Growth-Minded Individuals**

   - **Positive Influence:** Surround yourself with people who have a growth mindset. Their positive attitudes and behaviours can inspire and motivate you.
   - **Supportive Environment:** Create an environment that supports and encourages growth and learning. This can be achieved by joining groups, communities, or networks focused on personal development.

8. **Practice Gratitude**

   - **Appreciate Growth:** Regularly reflect on and appreciate the growth and progress you have made. Gratitude helps reinforce the positive aspects of your journey.

- o *Gratitude Journals:* Maintain a gratitude journal to document your experiences, learning, and achievements. This practice can help you stay focused on growth.

9. Develop Resilience

- o *Embrace Setbacks:* Understand that setbacks are a natural part of the growth process. Develop resilience by viewing setbacks as temporary and learning experiences.
- o *Persistence:* Cultivate persistence by continuing to work towards your goals despite difficulties. Remind yourself of past successes and how you overcame challenges.

10. Celebrate Effort and Progress

- *Recognition:* Regularly recognize and celebrate the effort and progress you make towards your goals. This reinforces the growth mindset and motivates further efforts.
- *Reward Systems:* Implement reward systems for achieving milestones and making progress. This can include small rewards or personal treats that acknowledge your hard work.

Practical Applications of a Growth Mindset

1. In Education

- o *Student Engagement:* Encourage students to adopt a growth mindset by emphasizing effort, resilience, and the value of learning from mistakes.
- o *Teaching Methods:* Implement teaching methods that promote active learning, critical thinking, and problem-solving skills.

2. **In the Workplace**

    o *Employee Development:* Foster a growth mindset culture by providing opportunities for continuous learning and professional development.

    o *Leadership:* Leaders should model a growth mindset by embracing challenges, seeking feedback, and promoting a learning-oriented environment.

3. **In Personal Life**

    o *Personal Goals*: Apply the growth mindset principles to personal goals, such as health, fitness, hobbies, and relationships.

    o *Self-Improvement*: Continuously seek ways to improve yourself and develop new skills and habits.

4. **In Relationships**

    o *Effective Communication*: Use growth mindset principles to enhance communication and resolve conflicts in relationships.

    o *Support and Encouragement:* Encourage and support growth and development in your relationships by fostering a positive and nurturing environment.

Final Thoughts: The Journey to a Growth-Oriented Life

Embarking on the journey to develop a growth mindset is a profound and transformative process that can positively influence every dimension of your life. By delving into the distinctions between a fixed and a growth mindset, appreciating the extensive advantages of adopting a growth mindset, and taking actionable steps to nurture it, you can unlock your ultimate potential and experience a higher degree of success and personal fulfilment.

The Profound Impact of a Growth Mindset

Cultivating a growth mindset involves more than just a shift in perspective; it represents a complete transformation in how you perceive your abilities, challenges, and potential. This journey begins with the realization that your talents and intelligence are not static but can be developed through dedication and hard work. This understanding lays the foundation for a mindset that embraces continuous learning and improvement.

Understanding Fixed vs. Growth Mindset

A fixed mindset, characterised by the belief that abilities are innate and unchangeable, often leads to a fear of failure and a reluctance to take on new challenges. In contrast, a growth mindset thrives on the belief that abilities can be honed and expanded through effort and perseverance. Recognizing these fundamental differences is crucial for anyone seeking to transition from a fixed to a growth mindset.

Recognizing the Benefits of a Growth Mindset

The benefits of a growth mindset are manifold and far-reaching. Individuals with a growth mindset are more likely to embrace challenges, persist in the face of setbacks, see effort as the path to mastery, and learn from criticism. This mindset fosters resilience, adaptability, and a proactive approach to problem-solving, which are essential traits for personal and professional success.

Implementing Practical Steps to Cultivate a Growth Mindset

Developing a growth mindset requires intentional effort and consistent practice. Here are several strategies to help you on this transformative journey:

1. **Embrace Challenges**: View challenges as opportunities to grow rather than as obstacles to avoid. Take on tasks that push your limits and expand your skills.
2. **Persist Through Setbacks**: Understand that setbacks and failures are part of the learning process. Use them as opportunities to learn and improve, rather than as reasons to give up.
3. **Value Effort Over Talent**: Focus on the effort you put into tasks rather than the innate talent you may or may not possess. Celebrate hard work and perseverance as much as you celebrate success.
4. **Learn from Criticism**: Instead of taking criticism personally, use it as a tool for growth. Reflect on feedback and apply it to improve your performance.
5. **Find Inspiration in Others' Success**: Instead of feeling threatened by the success of others, let it inspire you. Use their achievements as motivation to work harder and strive for your own success.

Becoming a Visionary Dreamer

Dreamers, those who envision possibilities beyond the present, play a pivotal role in inspiring and sustaining humanity. These visionaries dare to imagine a better future and work tirelessly to bring their dreams to fruition. By embracing a growth mindset, you too can become one of these dreamers. Your visions, nurtured through dedication and effort, can pave the way for innovation and progress.

The Role of Dedication and Effort

Achieving remarkable growth and transformation requires a commitment to continuous improvement. It demands that you dedicate time and effort to developing your skills and expanding your knowledge. With the right mindset, you can overcome challenges, learn from setbacks, and continually strive for excellence.

Making a Lasting Impact

By adopting a growth mindset, you not only transform your own life but also make a lasting impact on those around you. Your journey of growth and development can inspire others to embark on their own transformative journeys. Together, we can create a culture of continuous improvement and innovation, making the world a better place for future generations.

A Call to Action

Now is the time to embrace the growth mindset and embark on this transformative journey. Start by reflecting on your current mindset and identifying areas where you can adopt a more growth-oriented perspective. Implement the strategies outlined in this chapter and commit to continuous learning and improvement.

As you progress on this journey, remember that the path to a growth mindset is not always easy, but it is incredibly rewarding. With dedication, effort, and the right approach, you can achieve remarkable growth and transformation. Your dreams can become a reality!

Final Thoughts

Developing a growth mindset is not a destination but a continuous journey of self-improvement and learning. It is about recognizing your potential to grow, embracing challenges, and persistently striving for excellence. By adopting this mindset, you can unlock your full potential and achieve greater success and fulfilment in all areas of your life.

Embrace the dreamer within you and let your visions guide you toward a brighter future. With the right mindset, dedication, and effort, you can achieve remarkable growth and transformation, making a lasting impact on yourself and the world around you. The journey to a growth-oriented life begins now.

5

Daily Habits for Success

Character is built in the same way as a tree or a house is built—namely by the ceaseless addition of new material, and that material is thought.

Daily habits are the building blocks of our character and, ultimately, our future. Just as a tree grows by continually adding new rings and a house is constructed brick by brick, our character and success are shaped by the thoughts and actions we consistently engage in. The power of habits cannot be overstated, as they form the foundation upon which we build our lives. This chapter delves into the importance of daily habits, explores the routines of successful individuals, and provides strategies for building and sustaining productive habits.

"*Man is the doer of his own deeds; as such, he is the maker of his own character; and as the doer of his deeds and the maker of his character, he is the molder and shaper of his destiny.*" These profound words encapsulate the essence of human potential and the power of our actions. In the grand tapestry of life, change is the only constant. How we respond to change determines the trajectory of our lives. Embracing change and developing adaptability are essential skills that allow us to navigate the complexities of life, seize opportunities, and thrive amidst uncertainty.

The Inevitability of Change

Change is an inherent part of the human experience. From the moment we are born, we are subjected to a continuous stream of changes—some predictable, others unexpected. Whether it is the progression from infancy to adulthood, the shifts in our personal and professional lives, or the broader societal and technological transformations, change is inevitable. Understanding and accepting this inevitability is the first step towards developing a mindset that welcomes change rather than resists it.

Understanding Change

1. **Types of Change**
    - *Personal Change*: This includes changes in our personal lives such as moving to a new city, changes in relationships, or personal growth and development.
    - *Professional Change*: Changes in the workplace, career shifts, or advancements in technology that impact how we work.
    - *Societal Change*: Broader changes in society including cultural shifts, economic fluctuations, and political transformations.
    - *Global Change:* Changes that affect the entire world such as climate change, global pandemics, and international relations.

2. **The Psychological Impact of Change**
    - *Fear and Anxiety:* Change often brings with it fear of the unknown and anxiety about the future. These emotions are natural responses to uncertainty.

- o ***Resistance to Change***: Human beings have a natural tendency to resist change, preferring the comfort and familiarity of the status quo.
- o ***Embracing Change***: Developing a positive attitude towards change and viewing it as an opportunity for growth and improvement.

Strategies to Become Adaptable

1. Cultivating a Growth Mindset

- o ***Embrace Learning:*** See change as an opportunity to learn new skills and acquire new knowledge. Continuous learning helps in adapting to new situations.
- o ***View Challenges as Opportunities:*** Instead of seeing challenges as obstacles, view them as opportunities to grow and develop resilience.

2. Developing Emotional Resilience

- o ***Emotional Awareness:*** Being aware of your emotions and understanding how they impact your response to change.
- o ***Stress Management:*** Develop healthy ways to manage stress such as exercise, meditation, and relaxation techniques.

3. Building Flexibility into Your Routine

- o **Plan for Uncertainty:** While planning is important, it is equally important to be flexible and adaptable when things do not go as planned.
- o ***Be Open to New Experiences:*** Actively seek out new experiences and be willing to step out of your comfort zone.

4. **Enhancing Problem-Solving Skills**

    o *Critical Thinking:* Develop the ability to analyse situations critically and come up with creative solutions.

    o *Collaboration:* Work with others to solve problems. Collaboration often leads to better solutions and helps in adapting to change.

5. **Staying Physically and Mentally Fit**

    o *Healthy Lifestyle*: Maintain a healthy lifestyle with regular exercise, a balanced diet, and sufficient sleep.

    o *Mental Fitness:* Engage in activities that keep your mind sharp such as reading, puzzles, and continuous learning.

6. **Maintaining a Positive Outlook**

    o *Optimism:* Maintain an optimistic outlook and focus on the positive aspects of change.

    o *Gratitude*: Practice gratitude to maintain a positive attitude and appreciate the good things in life.

Stories of Individuals Who Thrived Through Change

1. **Howard Schultz: Brewing Success Amidst Challenges**

    o *Early Struggles:* Howard Schultz grew up in a poor family and faced significant financial hardships. Despite these challenges, he pursued a college education and eventually entered the business world.

    o *Transforming Starbucks*: Schultz saw potential in a small coffee company called Starbucks. After initially facing resistance, he acquired the company and transformed it into a global coffeehouse chain, innovating with the idea of a café experience.

- **Legacy**: Schultz's ability to envision a new market and adapt to changing consumer preferences left a lasting impact on the coffee industry, making Starbucks a household name worldwide.

2. **Ralph Lauren: Fashioning a Global Empire**

    - **Early Life and Career**: Ralph Lauren, born Ralph Lifshitz, grew up in a working-class family. He started his fashion career selling ties and faced numerous challenges in a highly competitive industry.
    - **Building a Brand**: Lauren's innovative designs and vision for a lifestyle brand led to the creation of Polo Ralph Lauren. He expanded the brand into a global fashion empire, setting new standards in the industry.
    - **Enduring Impact**: Ralph Lauren's adaptability and creative vision have made him an iconic figure in fashion, influencing trends and setting benchmarks for style and quality.

3. **Ursula Burns: Breaking Barriers in Corporate America**

    - **Overcoming Early Obstacles**: Ursula Burns grew up in a housing project in New York City. Despite the odds, she excelled academically and pursued a degree in mechanical engineering.
    - **Rising Through the Ranks**: Burns started her career at Xerox as an intern and worked her way up to become the first African American woman to lead a Fortune 500 company. She navigated the company through a significant transformation, focusing on digital technology and services.
    - **Trailblazing Leadership**: Burns' resilience and innovative leadership have broken barriers and inspired

countless women and minorities to pursue careers in STEM and corporate leadership.

4. **Chris Gardner: From Homelessness to Financial Success**

    o   ***Early Hardships***: Chris Gardner faced severe challenges, including homelessness while trying to raise his young son. Despite these hardships, he remained determined to change his circumstances.

    o   ***Pursuing a Dream***: Gardner's persistence paid off when he secured a position as an intern at a prestigious stock brokerage firm. He eventually became a successful stockbroker and founded his own brokerage firm.

    o   ***Inspirational Journey:*** Gardner's story, chronicled in his autobiography and the film "The Pursuit of Happyness," highlights the power of determination and adaptability in overcoming extreme adversity to achieve success.

5. **Francois Pinault: Navigating the Luxuries of Change**

    o   ***Business Ventures:*** Francois Pinault began his career in the timber industry and faced various business challenges. He diversified his ventures and entered the luxury goods market.

    o   ***Building Kering:*** Pinault acquired several high-end brands, including Gucci, Yves Saint Laurent, and Balenciaga, transforming his company, Kering, into a leading global luxury group.

    o   ***Strategic Vision***: Pinault's ability to adapt to market changes and recognize the potential of luxury brands has established him as a formidable figure in the luxury goods industry, shaping consumer preferences and industry standards.

Practical Steps to Embrace Change

1. **Develop a Vision for Change**
   - *Clarify Your Goals:* Define clear goals for what you want to achieve through change.
   - *Visualize Success*: Visualize the successful implementation of change and the positive outcomes it will bring.

2. **Create a Change Plan**
   - *Identify Steps:* Break down the change process into manageable steps.
   - *Set Milestones:* Establish milestones to track your progress and stay motivated.

3. **Build a Support System**
   - *Seek Support*: Surround yourself with supportive individuals who encourage and motivate you.
   - *Leverage Resources:* Utilize available resources such as mentors, coaches, and support groups to navigate change.

4. **Stay Informed and Prepared**
   - *Research and Learn*: Stay informed about potential changes and prepare by learning new skills and acquiring knowledge.
   - *Anticipate Challenges*: Anticipate potential challenges and develop strategies to overcome them.

5. **Celebrate Successes**
   - *Acknowledge Achievements:* Celebrate your

achievements and progress, no matter how small.
- **Reflect on Growth**: Reflect on how far you've come and the growth you've experienced through the change process.

Embracing change and developing adaptability are essential skills for navigating the complexities of life and achieving long-term success. By understanding the inevitability of change, cultivating a growth mindset, and implementing practical strategies to become adaptable, you can transform challenges into opportunities for growth and innovation. The stories of individuals who have thrived through change serve as powerful reminders of the resilience and potential within each of us. As you embark on your journey to embrace change, remember that you are the doer of your deeds, the maker of your character, and the shaper of your destiny. With dedication, effort, and the right mindset, you can achieve remarkable growth.

The Power of Habits in Shaping the Future

1. **Habits Define Your Character**
    - ***Cumulative Effect:*** The small actions you take each day accumulate over time, significantly impacting your overall character and life trajectory.
    - ***Consistency:*** Consistent behaviours reinforce specific traits and characteristics, shaping who you become.

2. **Habits Influence Success**
    - ***Routine and Structure***: Habits create routine and structure, making it easier to achieve goals and maintain productivity.
    - ***Automaticity:*** When behaviours become habitual, they

require less conscious effort, freeing up mental energy for more complex tasks.

3. Habits Affect Health and Well-being

- *Physical Health:* Daily habits such as exercise, healthy eating, and sufficient sleep contribute to long-term physical health.
- *Mental Health:* Practices like mindfulness, gratitude, and positive thinking improve mental well-being and resilience.

4. Habits Drive Goal Achievement

- *Actionable Steps:* Breaking down goals into daily habits makes them more manageable and achievable.
- *Momentum:* Consistent habits build momentum, making it easier to stay motivated and continue progressing toward your goals.

Daily Routines of Successful People

1. Morning Routines

- *Tim Cook (CEO of Apple):* Tim Cook starts his day at 4:30 AM, reading emails and planning his day. He then heads to the gym for a workout, emphasizing the importance of physical health and early preparation.
- *Oprah Winfrey:* Oprah begins her day with 20 minutes of meditation, followed by a workout and a nutritious breakfast. She prioritises mental clarity and physical wellness.

2. Work Routines

- *Elon Musk (CEO of Tesla and SpaceX):* Elon Musk

structures his day into 5-minute blocks to maximize efficiency. He focuses on high-priority tasks and delegates whenever possible.
- **Sheryl Sandberg (former COO of Facebook):** Sheryl Sandberg schedules everything, including time for family and personal activities. She believes in setting clear boundaries and priorities.

3. **Evening Routines**
   - **Barack Obama:** Former President Barack Obama spends his evenings reading and reflecting. He also enjoys spending time with his family, emphasizing the importance of work-life balance.
   - **Arianna Huffington:** Arianna Huffington practices a digital detox before bed, avoiding screens for at least an hour before sleep. She engages in relaxing activities like reading and taking a warm bath.

4. **Mindfulness and Reflection**
   - **Dalai Lama:** The Dalai Lama begins his day with several hours of prayer and meditation. He believes in the power of mindfulness and self-reflection for mental clarity and inner peace.
   - **Ray Dalio (Founder of Bridgewater Associates):** Ray Dalio practices transcendental meditation twice a day. He attributes much of his success to this habit, which helps him maintain focus and reduce stress.

How to Build and Sustain Productive Habits

1. **Start Small**
   - **Micro-Habits:** Begin with small, manageable habits that

are easy to incorporate into your daily routine. For example, if you want to start exercising, begin with a 5-minute walk each day.

- o *Gradual Increase:* Gradually increase the intensity and duration of the habit as it becomes more ingrained in your routine.

2. **Set Clear Goals**

    - o *Specificity:* Define clear, specific goals for your habits. Instead of saying, "I want to read more," specify, "I want to read for 20 minutes every day."
    - o *Measurable:* Ensure your goals are measurable so you can track your progress. For instance, aim to read a certain number of books per month.

3. **Create a Routine**

    - o *Consistency:* Establish a consistent routine for your habits. Performing the habit at the same time each day reinforces its place in your schedule.
    - o *Environment:* Design your environment to support your habits. For example, place your workout clothes next to your bed to remind you to exercise in the morning.

4. **Use Triggers and Cues**

    - o *Triggers:* Identify triggers that prompt your habits. For example, if you want to develop a habit of drinking more water, use meal times as triggers to remind you to drink a glass of water.
    - o *Cues:* Create visual or auditory cues to reinforce your habits. Setting an alarm or placing sticky notes in strategic locations can serve as reminders.

5. **Leverage Accountability**

    o *Accountability Partners*: Share your goals with a friend, family member, or mentor who can hold you accountable and provide support.

    o *Public Commitment:* Make a public commitment to your habit, such as posting about it on social media or joining a group with similar goals.

6. **Track Your Progress**

    o *Habit Trackers:* Use habit-tracking apps or journals to record your progress and maintain motivation.

    o *Reflect and Adjust:* Regularly review your progress and make adjustments as needed. Reflect on what is working and what challenges you face.

7. **Reward Yourself**

    o *Immediate Rewards:* Provide yourself with small, immediate rewards for completing your habit. This positive reinforcement can increase motivation.

    o *Milestone Rewards:* Set larger rewards for reaching significant milestones. For example, treat yourself to a special activity or purchase when you achieve a long-term goal.

8. **Overcome Obstacles**

    o *Identify Barriers*: Recognize potential obstacles that may hinder your habit formation and develop strategies to overcome them.

    o *Plan for Challenges:* Anticipate challenges and create contingency plans. For example, if you miss a workout, plan a makeup session the next day.

9. **Maintain Flexibility**

    o *Adaptation*: Be flexible and willing to adapt your habits as needed. Life circumstances may change, requiring adjustments to your routine.
    o *Persistence*: Stay persistent even when faced with setbacks. Remember that habit formation is a gradual process, and occasional lapses are normal.

10. **Integrate Habits into Your Identity**

    - *Identity-Based Habits:* Align your habits with your identity and values. For example, instead of saying, "I want to run," say, "I am a runner."
    - *Self-Image:* Cultivate a self-image that supports your habits. Visualize yourself as the person you want to become and act accordingly.

Practical Applications of Daily Habits

1. **Health and Fitness**

    o *Exercise Routine:* Establish a daily exercise routine that fits your lifestyle and preferences. Consistency is key to maintaining physical health.
    o *Healthy Eating:* Develop habits around healthy eating, such as meal prepping, choosing nutritious foods, and practising mindful eating.
    o *Sleep Hygiene*: Prioritise good sleep hygiene by creating a relaxing bedtime routine, maintaining a regular sleep schedule, and minimizing screen time before bed.

2. **Professional Growth**

    o *Skill Development:* Dedicate time each day to developing

professional skills, such as reading industry-related articles, taking courses, or practising new techniques.
- ***Networking:*** Build a habit of networking by reaching out to colleagues, attending industry events, and engaging in professional communities.

3. **Personal Development**
   - ***Mindfulness Practice:*** Incorporate mindfulness practices, such as meditation or journaling, into your daily routine to enhance mental clarity and emotional well-being.
   - ***Lifelong Learning:*** Commit to lifelong learning by setting aside time each day for reading, studying, or exploring new interests.

4. **Relationship Building**
   - ***Quality Time:*** Make it a habit to spend quality time with loved ones, whether through shared activities, meaningful conversations, or simple gestures of appreciation.
   - ***Active Listening:*** Practice active listening in your interactions, giving full attention and showing empathy and understanding.

5. **Financial Management**
   - ***Budgeting:*** Develop a habit of budgeting and tracking expenses to maintain financial stability and achieve long-term financial goals.
   - ***Saving and Investing:*** Make regular saving and investing a part of your routine to build wealth and secure your financial future.

Daily habits are the building blocks of success, shaping your character, health, relationships, and overall life trajectory. By understanding the power of habits, learning from the routines of successful individuals, and implementing strategies to build and sustain productive habits, you can create a foundation for long-term success and fulfilment. Remember, character is built through the ceaseless addition of new material—thoughts and actions that, over time, define who you are and what you achieve. Embrace the power of daily habits, and you will be well on your way to building a successful and fulfilling life.

THE EVOLUTION OF ADAPTABILITY: CHARTING NEW TERRITORIES

Understanding the Dynamics of Change

As we continue to explore the theme of adaptability, it is essential to delve deeper into the dynamic nature of change and how it influences every aspect of our lives. Change, by its very nature, disrupts the status quo and compels us to reassess our assumptions, beliefs, and behaviours. This disruption, while often uncomfortable, is the catalyst for growth and innovation. To navigate this ever-changing landscape, we must develop a keen understanding of the forces that drive change and how we can harness them to our advantage.

Identifying the Drivers of Change

1. **Technological Advancements**

   o *Rapid Innovation:* The pace of technological innovation has accelerated exponentially, transforming industries and reshaping the way we live and work. From artificial intelligence and robotics to blockchain and quantum computing, these advancements create new opportunities

and challenges that require continuous adaptation.
- o **_Digital Transformation_**: Businesses and individuals must embrace digital transformation to stay competitive. This includes adopting new technologies, optimizing processes, and leveraging data analytics to drive decision-making and enhance customer experiences.

2. **Globalization and Interconnectivity**

   - o **_Global Markets:_** The globalization of markets has opened up unprecedented opportunities for trade and collaboration. However, it also brings increased competition and the need for businesses to adapt to diverse cultural and regulatory environments.
   - o **_Cross-Cultural Communication_**: Effective communication across cultures is crucial in a globalized world. Developing cultural intelligence and adaptability allows individuals to navigate different social and business contexts successfully.

3. **Environmental and Social Changes**

   - o **_Climate Change:_** The impact of climate change necessitates significant shifts in how we manage resources, develop infrastructure, and plan for the future. Adaptability is key to mitigating risks and building resilience against environmental challenges.
   - o **_Social Movements:_** Social movements advocating for equality, justice, and sustainability are reshaping societal norms and expectations. Embracing these changes requires a willingness to listen, learn, and act in ways that promote positive social impact.

Strategies for Cultivating Adaptability

1. **Fostering a Learning Culture**

    o *Lifelong Learning:* Encourage a culture of lifelong learning where individuals continuously seek knowledge and skills. This can be achieved through formal education, professional development, and self-directed learning.

    o *Curiosity and Experimentation:* Cultivate curiosity and a willingness to experiment with new ideas and approaches. This mindset fosters innovation and adaptability by allowing individuals to explore diverse perspectives and solutions.

2. **Enhancing Emotional Intelligence**

    o *Self-Awareness:* Develop self-awareness to understand how emotions influence thoughts and behaviours. This awareness helps individuals manage their responses to change and maintain a positive outlook.

    o *Empathy and Social Skills*: Strengthen empathy and social skills to build strong relationships and support networks. These skills are vital for collaborating effectively and navigating interpersonal dynamics during times of change.

3. **Building Agile Organisations**

    o *Agile Methodologies:* Implement agile methodologies that prioritise flexibility, collaboration, and rapid iteration. Agile frameworks, such as Scrum and Kanban, enable organisations to respond quickly to changing market conditions and customer needs.

o ***Decentralized Decision-Making:*** Empower teams with the autonomy to make decisions and take action. Decentralized decision-making enhances responsiveness and innovation by leveraging the collective expertise of the organisation.

4. Developing a Resilient Mindset

o ***Positive Reframing:*** Practice positive reframing by viewing challenges as opportunities for growth. This mindset shift reduces stress and increases motivation to overcome obstacles.

o ***Mindfulness and Stress Management:*** Incorporate mindfulness practices and stress management techniques to maintain mental and emotional well-being. These practices enhance resilience by promoting clarity, focus, and calmness.

Case Studies of Adaptability in Action

1. Howard Schultz: Reinventing the Coffee Experience

o ***Visionary Leadership:*** Howard Schultz's vision to transform Starbucks from a coffee retailer to a community-centric café revolutionized the coffee industry. His ability to anticipate and adapt to changing consumer preferences played a crucial role in Starbucks' global success.

o ***Innovation and Growth:*** Schultz continuously innovated the Starbucks experience by introducing new products, expanding the brand's digital presence, and enhancing customer engagement. His adaptability ensured that Starbucks remained relevant and competitive in a dynamic market.

2. **Ralph Lauren: Crafting a Timeless Brand**

   o *Brand Evolution:* Ralph Lauren's ability to evolve his brand while maintaining its core identity has been a testament to his adaptability. From introducing new product lines to expanding into international markets, Lauren's strategic vision has driven the brand's enduring success.

   o *Sustainability Initiatives:* In response to growing consumer demand for sustainability, Ralph Lauren has integrated eco-friendly practices into the brand's operations. This adaptability reflects a commitment to aligning business practices with evolving societal values.

3. **Ursula Burns: Leading Through Transformation**

   o *Transformative Leadership:* Ursula Burns' leadership at Xerox exemplified adaptability during times of significant change. She guided the company through a major transformation, shifting its focus from manufacturing to digital services.

   o *Diversity and Inclusion*: Burns' advocacy for diversity and inclusion has been a cornerstone of her leadership. By fostering an inclusive culture, she enabled Xerox to attract diverse talent and drive innovation.

4. **Chris Gardner: Navigating Life's Challenges**

   o *Overcoming Adversity*: Chris Gardner's journey from homelessness to financial success underscores the power of resilience and adaptability. His unwavering determination and ability to adapt to changing circumstances paved the way for his achievements.

   o *Inspiring Others*: Gardner's story, depicted in "The

Pursuit of Happyness," has inspired countless individuals to persevere through their challenges. His adaptability serves as a powerful example of how to navigate and overcome life's obstacles.

5. **Francois Pinault: Redefining Luxury**

    o *Strategic Acquisitions*: Francois Pinault's strategic acquisitions of luxury brands have transformed Kering into a global leader in the luxury goods industry. His ability to identify and integrate diverse brands showcases his adaptability and business acumen.

    o *Embracing Sustainability*: Pinault's commitment to sustainability has reshaped Kering's operations and brand ethos. By prioritising environmental and social responsibility, he has aligned the company with contemporary consumer values and industry trends.

Practical Steps for Embracing Change

1. Anticipate Change

    o *Trend Analysis*: Regularly analyse industry trends and market signals to anticipate changes. This proactive approach enables individuals and organisations to prepare and adapt ahead of time.

    o *Scenario Planning*: Engage in scenario planning to explore potential future developments and their implications. This strategic exercise helps build resilience by considering various outcomes and preparing for uncertainties.

2. Embrace Continuous Improvement

    o *Kaizen Philosophy*: Adopt the Kaizen philosophy of

continuous improvement, which emphasizes incremental changes and ongoing refinement of processes. This approach fosters adaptability by encouraging constant learning and enhancement.
- *Feedback Loops:* Establish feedback loops to gather insights and refine strategies. Continuous feedback from customers, employees, and stakeholders informs decision-making and drives iterative improvements.

3. Develop a Change-Ready Culture

- *Change Champions*: Identify and empower change champions within the organisation who advocate for and lead change initiatives. These individuals can drive cultural shifts and foster a positive attitude towards change.
- *Training and Development:* Invest in training and development programs that equip individuals with the skills and knowledge needed to navigate change effectively. This investment builds a capable and adaptable workforce.

4. Maintain Flexibility

- *Flexible Structures*: Design organisational structures that are flexible and adaptable to change. This includes creating cross-functional teams and fluid roles that can respond to evolving needs.
- *Resource Allocation*: Allocate resources in a way that allows for quick adjustments. Having flexible budgets and resource pools enables organisations to pivot and capitalize on new opportunities.

5. **Leverage Technology**
    - *Digital Tools:* Utilize digital tools and platforms that enhance adaptability. Technologies such as artificial intelligence, cloud computing, and collaboration software facilitate agility and innovation.
    - *Data-Driven Decisions:* Leverage data analytics to make informed decisions and predict trends. Data-driven insights provide a solid foundation for adapting strategies and optimizing outcomes.

Final Thoughts: The Power of Adaptability

The journey of embracing change and developing adaptability is one of continuous evolution. By understanding the dynamics of change, cultivating resilience, and implementing strategic approaches, individuals and organisations can navigate the complexities of the modern world with confidence. The stories of visionary leaders like Howard Schultz, Ralph Lauren, Ursula Burns, Chris Gardner, and Francois Pinault highlight the transformative power of adaptability in achieving success and making a lasting impact.

As we move forward, it is essential to recognize that adaptability is not a one-time effort but an ongoing commitment to growth and improvement. By fostering a mindset that welcomes change, building flexible structures, and leveraging technology, we can create a future that is resilient, innovative, and full of possibilities. Embrace the journey of adaptability, and you will discover the limitless potential within yourself and your organisation, ready to thrive in an ever-changing world.

6

Embracing Change and Adaptability

Man is the creator of his own actions; in doing so, he shapes his character. Through these actions and the character he builds, he becomes the architect of his own fate.

These profound words emphasize the boundless power we possess over the trajectory of our lives. Each decision we make, each action we take, contributes to the ongoing formation of our character and ultimately sculpts our destiny.

In the intricate tapestry of life, change is the singular constant. It permeates every aspect of our existence, influencing the minutiae of our daily routines as well as the sweeping arcs of our life narratives. Our capacity to manage and adapt to change is a crucial determinant of our overall success and sense of fulfilment. Embracing change and fostering adaptability are essential skills for thriving in a world perpetually in flux.

EMBRACING THE DANCE OF CHANGE: A WHIMSICAL GUIDE TO NAVIGATING LIFE'S TWISTS AND TURNS

The Cha-Cha of Change

Change is the name of the game, folks! It's as inevitable as your favourite TV show getting canceled right when it gets good. It comes in all shapes and sizes—tech breakthroughs, societal shifts, economic rollercoasters, personal epiphanies, and those curveballs life loves to throw our way. Whether it's a slow waltz or a quickstep, understanding the many faces of change is your ticket to mastering it.

Technological Advancements: The Tech Tango

Ah, technology! It's like that dance partner who keeps stepping on your toes but also takes you to new heights. Remember when the internet was just a weird noise your computer made? Now we've got smartphones smarter than most of us! Embracing these digital leaps and bounds keeps you grooving at the forefront of progress.

Social Shifts: The Cultural Conga

Society loves a good conga line, constantly moving and evolving. What was considered cool or acceptable ten years ago might make you a meme today. Stay attuned to these cultural rhythms, adjust your steps, and you'll navigate the modern dance floor with grace and style.

Economic Fluctuations: The Financial Foxtrot

The economy is the ultimate dance marathon, with twists, turns, and unexpected dips. Market trends, financial crises, and economic booms keep us all on our toes. Learning the steps of financial literacy and resilience can help you dance through these economic swings with confidence and poise.

Personal Transformations: The Life Lambada

On a personal level, change can feel like the sultry lambada, full of passion and unpredictability. From career changes to relationship dynamics and health challenges, each experience shapes our character. Embrace these personal transformations with an open mind and a positive attitude, and watch yourself grow into a seasoned dancer of life.

THE INEVITABILITY OF CHANGE: THE ETERNAL FLOW

Nature of Change: The Constant Flux

Life is in constant motion, a never-ending dance of change. From personal growth to the latest tech, everything around us is in flux. Some changes we can predict, while others sneak up on us like a surprise dance partner. Being ready to adapt quickly is key.

Change in Personal Life: The Rhythm of Life Stages

As we move through life—childhood, adolescence, adulthood, and the golden years—our priorities, responsibilities, and perspectives change. Relationships also evolve, be they friendships, romances, or family dynamics. Staying in tune with these shifts helps us navigate life's complex choreography.

Change in Professional Life: The Career Quickstep

Careers rarely follow a straight path. Job changes, promotions, and career pivots are the norm in today's workforce. Industries evolve due to technological advancements and market trends. Continuous learning and adaptation keep you in the professional dance.

Change in the External Environment: The Global Waltz

Global events, from political shifts to economic changes and environmental crises, have profound effects on individuals and communities. Rapid technological progress impacts how we communicate, work, and live. Staying informed and flexible helps you keep in step with these global rhythms.

So, there you have it! Life is one big, unpredictable dance floor. Embrace the music of change, find your rhythm, and remember—it's not about having perfect moves but enjoying the dance itself.

MASTERING THE ART OF ADAPTABILITY: A FUN GUIDE TO THRIVING IN A WORLD OF CHANGE

Strategies to Become Adaptable

1. Cultivate a Growth Mindset: The "I Can Do It" Dance

- *Embrace Learning:* View every challenge and change as a dance move to learn. The more you practice, the better you get. Stay open to new steps and rhythms!
- *Positive Attitude:* Keep your chin up and your spirits high. See change as an exciting opportunity to groove to a new beat rather than a scary unknown.

2. Enhance Emotional Intelligence: The Feel-Good Groove

- *Self-Awareness:* Know your own dance style—understand your emotions and how you react to change. Spot your strengths and areas where you might trip up.

- ***Empathy:*** Tune into others' vibes. Understanding and supporting your fellow dancers fosters harmony and teamwork on the dance floor of life.

3. Build Resilience: The Bounce-Back Boogie

- ***Stress Management:*** Keep your cool with mindfulness, meditation, and a good workout. These are your go-to moves for staying mentally and emotionally fit.
- ***Persistence:*** Don't let a few missteps stop you. Build resilience by bouncing back from setbacks, ready to tackle the next routine.

4. Stay Flexible: The Adaptable Samba

- ***Adaptability:*** Be ready to switch up your steps and strategies as the music changes. Flexibility keeps you moving smoothly through life's unpredictable rhythms.
- ***Open-Mindedness:*** Stay curious and open to new ideas. Being receptive to different beats and perspectives helps you navigate various situations with ease.

5. Develop Problem-Solving Skills: The Brainy Breakdance

- ***Critical Thinking:*** Sharpen your critical thinking skills to analyse the dance floor, spot problems, and come up with effective solutions.
- ***Creativity:*** Think outside the box to come up with innovative moves and solutions to challenges. Creativity is your secret weapon!

6. Set Realistic Goals: The Goal-Setting Glide

- ***Short-Term Goals:*** Break it down! Set achievable short-term goals that keep you motivated and aligned with your long-term vision.

- **Adjust Goals:** Be ready to tweak your goals as needed. Flexibility in goal-setting helps you adapt to changing circumstances and keeps you on track.

7. Seek Support: The Buddy Boogie

- **Mentorship:** Find mentors who have mastered the art of navigating change. Their insights and advice are like having a seasoned dance coach.
- **Support Networks:** Build a strong crew of friends, family, and colleagues who can provide encouragement and assistance when you need it most.

8. Practice Self-Care: The Self-Love Salsa

- **Physical Health:** Keep your body in top shape with regular exercise, a balanced diet, and enough sleep. A healthy body supports a resilient mind.
- **Mental Health:** Prioritise your mental well-being by engaging in activities that reduce stress and promote relaxation. Seek professional help if needed.

ENHANCING ADAPTABILITY: THE BIG PICTURE

Practising Mindfulness and Self-Awareness

Mindfulness keeps you grounded in the present, fully aware of your thoughts, feelings, and surroundings. Self-awareness helps you understand your dance style, recognize your strengths, and spot areas for improvement. Together, they make you more responsive to change and new opportunities.

Building a Support Network

Having a strong support network is like having a dance troupe backing you up. Friends, family, mentors, and colleagues provide valuable perspectives, emotional support, practical advice, and diverse viewpoints that enhance your ability to adapt.

Continuous Learning

In a world that's always changing, continuous learning keeps you on your toes. Seek out new knowledge, skills, and experiences through formal education, professional development, or personal hobbies. A commitment to lifelong learning ensures you stay agile and ready to embrace whatever comes your way.

So, lace up those dancing shoes and get ready to master the art of adaptability. Remember, it's not about being the best dancer but enjoying the dance of life with all its twists, turns, and unexpected dips!

INSPIRATIONAL STORIES OF ADAPTABILITY AND SUCCESS

Larry Ellison: The Visionary

Background: Larry Ellison was born to a single mother and raised by his aunt and uncle in a modest Chicago neighbourhood. His early life was marked by struggles, including health issues and financial instability.

Adaptability: Despite these challenges, Ellison showed a remarkable ability to adapt and seize opportunities. He dropped out of college twice but continued to educate himself in computing and software engineering. His resilience and innovative thinking led him to co-found Oracle Corporation in 1977.

Outcome: Under his leadership, Oracle became a dominant force in the technology industry, pioneering database software solutions that revolutionized business operations worldwide.

Ellison's adaptability and visionary leadership have made him one of the wealthiest and most influential figures in tech.

Roman Abramovich: The Mogul

Background: Orphaned at a young age, Roman Abramovich was raised by relatives in a poor area of Russia. He faced significant hardships, including the instability of the post-Soviet economy.

Adaptability: Abramovich demonstrated remarkable business acumen and adaptability, starting with small-scale enterprises and gradually expanding into the oil industry. His strategic investments and ability to navigate the volatile market conditions enabled him to amass substantial wealth.

Outcome: Abramovich became a billionaire and is best known for his ownership of Chelsea Football Club, transforming it into one of the most successful football teams in the world. His story is a testament to the power of adaptability and strategic thinking in overcoming adversity.

Sam Walton: The Retail Pioneer

Background: Growing up during the Great Depression, Sam Walton worked various jobs to support his family. His early experiences with hardship and financial struggle shaped his work ethic and entrepreneurial spirit.

Adaptability: Walton's adaptability was evident as he explored different business opportunities and learned from each experience. He founded Walmart in 1962, applying innovative business practices such as supply chain optimization and aggressive pricing strategies.

Outcome: Walmart grew into the largest retailer in the world, revolutionizing the retail industry and making Walton one of the richest individuals in history. His legacy continues to influence modern retail practices and business strategies.

Steve Jobs: The Innovator

Background: Adopted and raised in a modest family, Steve Jobs co-founded Apple in his parents' garage. Despite facing numerous challenges, including being ousted from the company he helped create, Jobs remained resilient and innovative.

Adaptability: Jobs embraced change by founding NeXT and Pixar, which led to significant innovations in technology and entertainment. His ability to learn from setbacks and continually reinvent himself was key to his success.

Outcome: Jobs returned to Apple, leading a period of unprecedented growth and innovation, resulting in iconic products like the iPhone and iPad. His visionary leadership and adaptability have left an indelible mark on multiple industries.

John Paul DeJoria: The Entrepreneur

Background: John Paul DeJoria faced significant hardships, including homelessness and financial instability. Despite these challenges, he co-founded John Paul Mitchell Systems with just $700.

Adaptability: DeJoria's resilience and adaptability were crucial in overcoming the obstacles he faced. He later founded Patron Spirits Company, applying his entrepreneurial skills to a new industry.

Outcome: DeJoria amassed significant wealth and became a philanthropist, using his success to give back to the community. His story is a powerful example of how adaptability and perseverance can lead to extraordinary success.

Do Won Chang: The Fashion Tycoon

Background: Immigrating to the United States from South Korea with little money, Do Won Chang and his wife faced numerous challenges in their new country. They worked multiple jobs to make ends meet.

Adaptability: Chang's adaptability was evident as he and his wife started Forever 21 with a small storefront. They leveraged their understanding of fashion trends and consumer behaviour to grow their business.

Outcome: Forever 21 grew into a major international fashion retailer, known for its trendy and affordable clothing. Chang's story highlights the importance of adaptability and hard work in achieving the American Dream.

Li Ka-Shing: The Industrialist

Background: Fleeing to Hong Kong during wartime and working menial jobs, Li Ka-Shing faced significant adversity in his early life. His humble beginnings did not deter him from pursuing success.

Adaptability: Li's ability to adapt and seize opportunities was key to his success. He founded Cheung Kong Industries, starting with plastic manufacturing and eventually expanding into real estate and other sectors.

Outcome: Li became one of the richest men in Asia, known for his diversified business empire and philanthropic efforts. His adaptability and entrepreneurial spirit have made him a revered figure in the business world.

Guy Laliberté: The Entertainer

Background: Starting out as a street performer, Guy Laliberté faced numerous challenges in his early career. His passion for entertainment and creativity drove him to explore new possibilities.

Adaptability: Laliberté co-founded Cirque du Soleil, transforming it into a world-renowned entertainment company. His ability to innovate and adapt to changing audience preferences was crucial to the company's success.

Outcome: Cirque du Soleil became a global phenomenon, known for its unique blend of circus arts and theatrical performances. Laliberté's story is a testament to the power of creativity and adaptability in achieving extraordinary success.

Ralph De La Vega: The Telecommunications Leader

Background: Born in Cuba and arriving in the U.S. alone as a young boy, Ralph De La Vega faced significant challenges, including language barriers and cultural adjustment.

Adaptability: De La Vega's adaptability and determination helped him overcome these obstacles. He worked his way up from humble beginnings to become a key executive in the telecommunications industry.

Outcome: As the CEO of AT&T Mobility, De La Vega played a pivotal role in the company's growth and innovation. His story highlights the importance of adaptability and perseverance in achieving leadership success.

Ingvar Kamprad: The Furniture Innovator

Background: Growing up on a small farm in Sweden, Ingvar

Kamprad faced numerous challenges, including financial constraints. His entrepreneurial spirit was evident from a young age.

Adaptability: Kamprad founded IKEA at a young age, applying innovative business practices such as flat-pack furniture and self-assembly to reduce costs and increase accessibility.

Outcome: IKEA became the world's largest furniture retailer, known for its affordable and stylish products. Kamprad's adaptability and innovative approach have left a lasting impact on the global retail industry.

These stories of remarkable individuals demonstrate how adaptability, resilience, and an innovative mindset can lead to extraordinary success, regardless of the challenges one faces. Their journeys serve as powerful reminders of the potential within each of us to shape our own destinies through adaptability and perseverance.

As we navigate the complexities of life, our ability to adapt to change becomes a critical factor in shaping our destiny. By understanding the nature of change, cultivating adaptability, and drawing inspiration from those who have thrived through change, we empower ourselves to craft our own paths. Each decision we make, every action we take, contributes to the continuous formation of our character and ultimately molds our fate. Embracing change and fostering adaptability are not merely survival strategies; they are the keys to thriving in an ever-evolving world.

In this journey of crafting our own paths, we become the creators of our actions, the shapers of our character, and the architects of our destiny. The power to change, adapt, and thrive lies within each of us. By harnessing this power, we can navigate the currents of change with confidence and purpose, ultimately leading us to a life of fulfilment and success.

PRACTICAL APPLICATIONS OF ADAPTABILITY: A DEEP DIVE INTO EVERY ASPECT OF LIFE

1. In Personal Life

Navigating Relationships

Relationships are like delicate ecosystems; they require constant care, attention, and a good dose of adaptability to thrive. In romantic partnerships, flexibility means being open to your partner's evolving needs and dreams. It means navigating the ups and downs with grace, finding compromise, and growing together rather than apart.

Friendships, too, demand adaptability. As we journey through different life stages—school, work, parenthood, retirement—our time, interests, and priorities shift. Adaptable friends understand and embrace these changes, keeping the bond strong despite the inevitable ebbs and flows of life.

Family relationships can be particularly challenging, with their deep-rooted dynamics and history. Being adaptable here means being willing to see things from another's perspective, to forgive and move forward, and to adjust our expectations as family members grow and change. This kind of adaptability can transform family conflicts into opportunities for deeper connection and understanding.

Personal Growth

Personal growth is the essence of a fulfilling life, and adaptability is its cornerstone. Embracing change means constantly learning and evolving. It means being willing to step out of your comfort zone, to tackle new challenges, and to learn from failures rather than be defeated by them.

Consider the process of acquiring a new skill, such as learning a language or picking up a musical instrument. Adaptability enables you to navigate the initial clumsiness and frustration, to persevere through the steep learning curve, and to eventually master the new ability. This not only enriches your life with new experiences but also boosts your confidence and sense of achievement.

Adaptability also plays a crucial role in mental and emotional health. Life's unpredictable nature means we will inevitably face setbacks, losses, and disappointments. Those who can adapt to these challenges, who can find new paths when old ones are blocked, are more likely to maintain a positive outlook and a sense of purpose.

2. In Professional Life

Career Development

In the rapidly changing landscape of the modern workplace, adaptability is not just an asset; it is a necessity. Career paths are no longer linear; they are dynamic, with frequent shifts and turns. Whether it's moving to a new job, seeking a promotion, or completely changing career directions, adaptability is key.

Being adaptable means staying open to learning new skills and technologies, even if they are outside your current expertise. It means being willing to take on new roles and responsibilities, to continuously update your knowledge base, and to network with a diverse range of professionals. This not only makes you more marketable but also keeps your career engaging and fulfilling.

Leadership

Effective leadership in today's world is synonymous with

adaptability. Leaders must be able to respond swiftly to changes in the market, technology, and society. They must inspire their teams to embrace change, to innovate, and to continually seek improvement.

An adaptable leader fosters a culture of resilience within their organisation. They encourage open communication, where team members feel safe to express ideas and concerns. They promote continuous learning and development, ensuring that the team is always prepared to meet new challenges. In times of crisis, an adaptable leader remains calm, makes informed decisions, and guides the team through uncertainty with confidence and clarity.

3. In Business and Entrepreneurship

Market Trends

The business world is in a constant state of flux, driven by shifting market trends, evolving consumer behaviours, and rapid technological advancements. For businesses to stay competitive, adaptability is essential. This means being able to pivot strategies, update products and services, and explore new markets as conditions change.

Successful businesses often employ market research and data analysis to stay ahead of trends. They foster a culture of innovation, where employees are encouraged to experiment with new ideas and solutions. By being adaptable, businesses can not only survive but thrive in a constantly changing landscape.

Crisis Management

No business is immune to crises, be they economic downturns, natural disasters, or sudden market shifts. Adaptability is a critical component of effective crisis management. It involves quick decision-making, resourcefulness, and the ability to pivot operations to meet new demands.

For example, during the COVID-19 pandemic, many businesses had to quickly adapt to remote working conditions. Those that could swiftly implement new technologies, support their employees, and find innovative ways to serve their customers were able to weather the storm better than those that were rigid and slow to respond.

4. In Education

Learning Approaches

The field of education is undergoing significant transformation, driven by technological advancements and changing societal needs. Educators and students alike must be adaptable to benefit from these changes. This means embracing new technologies such as online learning platforms, interactive software, and digital resources.

For educators, adaptability involves continuously updating their teaching methods to meet the diverse needs of their students. It means being open to new pedagogical approaches, such as flipped classrooms or project-based learning, which can enhance student engagement and learning outcomes.

Lifelong Learning

Adaptability is also at the heart of lifelong learning. In a world where knowledge and skills quickly become outdated, the ability to continuously learn and adapt is crucial for personal and professional growth. This involves a commitment to seeking out new knowledge and skills throughout one's life, whether through formal education, professional development, or personal hobbies and interests.

Lifelong learners are adaptable by nature. They remain

curious, open-minded, and willing to step outside their comfort zones. This not only keeps their minds sharp but also allows them to adapt to changes in their careers and personal lives more effectively.

Adaptability is a multifaceted skill that touches every aspect of our lives. It is essential for navigating personal relationships, fostering personal growth, advancing in our careers, leading effectively, succeeding in business, and thriving in education. By cultivating adaptability, we equip ourselves to handle life's inevitable changes with grace and resilience, turning challenges into opportunities for growth and success. So, embrace the dance of change, keep learning, stay flexible, and watch as you navigate life with newfound confidence and joy.

Final Thoughts

Embracing change and developing adaptability are essential for navigating the complexities of life and achieving success. By understanding the inevitability of change, implementing strategies to become more adaptable, and learning from the experiences of individuals who have thrived through change, you can enhance your resilience and ability to handle any challenge. Remember, as the doer of your deeds and the maker of your character, you are the moulder and shaper of your destiny. Embrace change with an open mind and a positive attitude, and you will find opportunities for growth and success in every situation.

7

Building Strong Relationships

The Man Who is Continually Instructing Others Gratis How to Manage Their Affairs is the One Who Most Mismanages His Own: An In-Depth Exploration of Success Through Relationships

In the journey of life, one often encounters individuals who are quick to offer unsolicited advice, believing they possess the wisdom to guide others on how to navigate their personal and professional paths. However, it is frequently observed that those who are most eager to counsel others are the ones who struggle the most with managing their own affairs. This paradox is a testament to the complexity of human behaviour and the often-overlooked principle that true wisdom lies not just in knowing what to do, but in the ability to implement that knowledge effectively in one's own life.

The foundation of success often lies not just in individual effort but in the quality of relationships we build and maintain. Strong relationships, whether personal or professional, play a crucial role in shaping our lives and achievements. This chapter explores the importance of networking and relationships, strategies for building and maintaining professional relationships, and the impact of personal relationships on success.

The Foundation of Success: Beyond Individual Effort

Success is often perceived as a product of individual effort, talent, and determination. While these elements are undeniably important, they are not the sole determinants of success. The quality of relationships we build and maintain is a fundamental, yet sometimes underestimated, factor in achieving our goals. Whether in personal life or professional endeavours, strong relationships can provide support, open doors to new opportunities, and contribute to a sense of fulfilment and purpose.

The Importance of Networking and Relationships

Networking is not merely about collecting contacts; it's about planting relationships. The essence of networking lies in creating a web of connections that can offer mutual benefits. In a professional context, networking can lead to job opportunities, partnerships, mentorship, and access to resources that might otherwise be out of reach. Building a robust network requires authenticity, mutual respect, and the willingness to invest time and effort into nurturing these connections.

1. **Support System**

    o *Emotional Support:* Strong relationships provide emotional support, helping us navigate the ups and downs of life. Friends and family can offer comfort, encouragement, and perspective during challenging times.

    o *Professional Support:* In a professional context, relationships with mentors, colleagues, and industry peers can provide guidance, advice, and opportunities for career advancement.

2. **Opportunities for Growth**

     o   ***Career Advancement:*** Networking can open doors to new job opportunities, promotions, and professional development. Knowing the right people can significantly impact your career trajectory.

     o   ***Learning and Development:*** Interacting with others allows you to learn from their experiences and gain new insights. This continuous learning can enhance your skills and knowledge.

3. **Collaboration and Innovation**

     o   ***Teamwork:*** Effective collaboration often stems from strong relationships. Trust and mutual respect among team members lead to better communication and more productive teamwork.

     o   ***Innovation:*** Diverse perspectives and ideas from a wide network can drive innovation. Engaging with people from different backgrounds can spark creative solutions and new approaches.

4. **Reputation and Credibility**

     o   ***Building Trust:*** Strong relationships are built on trust. Being reliable and maintaining integrity in your interactions helps build a positive reputation.

     o   ***Credibility:*** Positive relationships with influential people in your industry can enhance your credibility and professional standing.

5. **Authenticity and Integrity**

     o   Be genuine in your interactions. People can sense insincerity, and authentic relationships are built on trust

and integrity.
- Example: In the film "The Pursuit of Happyness," Chris Gardner (played by Will Smith) exemplifies authenticity. His genuine nature and integrity earn him the trust and respect of his colleagues, eventually leading to his success.

6. **Active Listening**

    - Show genuine interest in others. Listen more than you speak and pay attention to what others are saying.
    - Example: In the book "How to Win Friends and Influence People" by Dale Carnegie, the importance of active listening is emphasized as a key strategy for building strong relationships.

7. **Providing Value**

    - Look for ways to add value to others' lives and careers without expecting immediate returns. This could be through sharing knowledge, offering assistance, or connecting them with valuable contacts.
    - Example: In "Pay It Forward" by Catherine Ryan Hyde, the protagonist, Trevor, creates a ripple effect of kindness and support by providing value to others without expecting anything in return.

8. **Consistency**

    - Maintain regular contact with your network. This doesn't mean pestering them but finding meaningful ways to stay in touch, whether through occasional emails, meetings, or social media interactions.
    - Example: In the film "Up in the Air," Ryan Bingham (played by George Clooney) illustrates the power of

consistent networking as he maintains a vast network of professional contacts through frequent travel and regular communication.

9. **Follow-Up**

    o   After meeting someone new, follow up with a personalized message. This helps cement the initial connection and opens the door for future interactions.
    o   Example: In "The Art of the Deal" by Donald Trump, the importance of following up is highlighted as a critical component of successful business negotiations and relationship-building.

Building and Maintaining Professional Relationships

1. **Show Appreciation**

    o   Acknowledge and appreciate the help and support you receive. A simple thank you can go a long way.
    o   Example: In "Thank You for Arguing" by Jay Heinrichs, the power of gratitude in maintaining relationships is discussed, showing how appreciation can strengthen bonds and build goodwill.

2. **Be Reliable**

    o   Honor your commitments and be someone others can depend on.
    o   Example: In "To Kill a Mockingbird" by Harper Lee, Atticus Finch's reliability and steadfastness earn him the respect and trust of the community.

3. **Stay Updated**

    o   Keep your network informed about your professional

progress and stay updated about theirs. Congratulate them on their achievements and support them in their endeavours.
- Example: In "Lean In" by Sheryl Sandberg, the importance of staying connected and updated with one's professional network is emphasized as a key strategy for career advancement.

4. Collaborate and Share Credit

- Collaborate on projects and share credit where it's due. This builds goodwill and strengthens professional bonds.
- Example: In "Team of Rivals" by Doris Kearns Goodwin, Abraham Lincoln's ability to collaborate and share credit with his rivals strengthened his leadership and achieved significant political success.

5. Handle Conflicts Gracefully

- In the professional world, conflicts are inevitable. Handle disagreements with grace and aim for constructive resolutions.
- Example: In "Crucial Conversations" by Kerry Patterson, the art of handling conflicts gracefully is explored, offering strategies for turning disagreements into productive discussions.

Personal Relationships and Their Impact on Success

1. Emotional Well-being

- ***Supportive Environment:*** Personal relationships provide a supportive environment that can enhance your emotional well-being. Positive relationships contribute to happiness and reduce stress.

- o ***Motivation:*** Loved ones can motivate and inspire you to pursue your goals. Their encouragement can boost your confidence and determination.

2. Work-Life Balance

- o ***Balancing Priorities:*** Strong personal relationships help you maintain a healthy work-life balance. They remind you of the importance of taking time for yourself and your loved ones.
- o ***Quality Time:*** Spending quality time with family and friends can rejuvenate you, leading to better productivity and creativity in your professional life.

3. Personal Growth

- o ***Feedback and Reflection:*** Personal relationships provide opportunities for feedback and reflection. Honest conversations with loved ones can help you grow and improve.
- o ***Shared Experiences:*** Sharing experiences with others enriches your life and broadens your perspective. This can lead to personal growth and a deeper understanding of yourself and others.

4. Conflict Resolution

- o ***Healthy Communication:*** Strong personal relationships teach you healthy communication skills that are valuable in resolving conflicts both personally and professionally.
- o ***Empathy and Understanding:*** Developing empathy and understanding in personal relationships can translate to better interactions and relationships at work.

5. Support in Adversity

- ***Resilience***: During challenging times, personal relationships provide a safety net that can help you bounce back. The support and encouragement of loved ones build resilience.
- ***Coping Mechanisms:*** Personal relationships offer coping mechanisms for dealing with stress and adversity. Whether it's talking through problems or simply being there, loved ones play a crucial role in navigating tough times.

Practical Applications of Building Strong Relationships

1. In Personal Life

- ***Quality Time***: Prioritise spending quality time with loved ones. Plan regular activities and create traditions that strengthen your bonds.
- ***Open Communication***: Maintain open lines of communication. Be honest, listen actively, and express your thoughts and feelings constructively.
- ***Acts of Kindness***: Show appreciation and kindness in your relationships. Small gestures, like a thoughtful note or a helping hand, can go a long way.

2. In Professional Life

- ***Networking Events***: Attend industry events, conferences, and seminars to expand your professional network. Engage with speakers and participants to build connections.
- ***Collaboration***: Foster a collaborative work environment by building strong relationships with colleagues. Work together on projects and support each other's professional growth.

- **Recognition**: Acknowledge and celebrate the achievements of your peers. Recognition strengthens relationships and builds a positive work culture.

3. **In Business and Entrepreneurship**

    - ***Customer Relationships***: Build strong relationships with your customers. Understand their needs, provide excellent service, and engage with them regularly.
    - ***Partnerships***: Develop strategic partnerships with other businesses. Collaborations can lead to new opportunities and mutual growth.
    - ***Community Engagement:*** Engage with your community through events, sponsorships, and volunteer work. Building a positive relationship with your community enhances your brand's reputation.

4. **In Education**

    - ***Student Relationships:*** Build strong relationships with students by showing genuine interest in their progress and well-being. Provide support and encouragement.
    - ***Professional Development***: Develop relationships with colleagues and mentors in the educational field. Share resources, collaborate on projects, and support each other's development.
    - ***Parental Involvement:*** Foster strong relationships with parents to support student success. Communicate regularly and involve them in the educational process.

Effective Networking

- **Purposeful Networking**

    - Approach networking with a clear purpose. Identify the

key people and events that align with your career goals and interests.
- Example: In "Never Eat Alone" by Keith Ferrazzi, the author illustrates how purposeful networking can open doors to incredible opportunities and foster long-lasting relationships.

- **Authenticity**
  - Be genuine in your interactions. People appreciate authenticity and are more likely to respond positively to sincere efforts to connect.
  - Example: In "The Authenticity Principle" by Ritu Bhasin, the importance of bringing your true self to your interactions is highlighted as a pathway to building deeper connections.

- **Value Addition**
  - Focus on how you can add value to others. Offer help, share resources, and show genuine interest in their work and achievements.
  - Example: In "Give and Take" by Adam Grant, the concept of value addition is explored, demonstrating how helping others can lead to personal and professional success.

Communication Skills

- **Active Listening**
  - Practice active listening by giving your full attention, asking questions, and showing empathy. This helps build rapport and demonstrates respect.
  - Example: In "You're Not Listening" by Kate Murphy,

the power of active listening is dissected, revealing how it can transform relationships and communication.

- **Clarity and Conciseness**
  - Communicate clearly and concisely. Avoid jargon and be straightforward in your conversations to ensure your message is understood.
  - Example: In "On Writing Well" by William Zinsser, the importance of clear and concise communication is emphasized, offering practical advice for effective writing and speaking.

- **Follow-Up**
  - Follow up on your interactions. Send thank-you notes, keep in touch through regular updates, and show appreciation for the time and insights shared by others.
  - Example: In "The 7 Habits of Highly Effective People" by Stephen R. Covey, the habit of follow-up is linked to building and maintaining strong relationships.

Building Trust

- **Reliability**
  - Be reliable and keep your commitments. Consistently delivering on your promises builds trust and reinforces your credibility.
  - Example: In "Good to Great" by Jim Collins, the reliability of great leaders is highlighted as a cornerstone of successful companies.

- **Transparency**
  - Be transparent in your dealings. Honesty and openness

create a strong foundation for lasting relationships.
- o Example: In "Radical Transparency" by Ray Dalio, the principles of transparency and openness are discussed as essential elements of building trust within organisations.

- **Consistency**

  o Show consistency in your behaviour and interactions. Consistency reinforces trust and reliability.

  o Example: In "The Power of Consistency" by Weldon Long, the significance of consistency in achieving personal and professional success is explored.

Leveraging Social Media

- **Professional Platforms**

  o Use professional platforms like LinkedIn to connect with industry peers, share your work, and engage in meaningful discussions.

  o Example: In "The LinkedIn Code" by Melonie Dodaro, strategies for effectively using LinkedIn to build a professional network are outlined.

- **Personal Branding**

  o Build a strong personal brand by sharing valuable content, participating in relevant groups, and showcasing your expertise.

  o Example: In "Crushing It!" by Gary Vaynerchuk, the importance of personal branding on social media is emphasized, providing tips for establishing a powerful online presence.

- **Engagement**
  - Actively engage with your network by commenting on posts, sharing insights, and acknowledging others' achievements.
  - Example: In "Digital Minimalism" by Cal Newport, the concept of meaningful engagement on social media is discussed, highlighting how to use digital platforms effectively without being overwhelmed.

Mentorship and Coaching

- **Finding a Mentor**
  - Seek mentors who can provide guidance, advice, and support. Mentors can offer valuable insights based on their experiences and help you navigate your career path.
  - Example: In "The Mentor Leader" by Tony Dungy, the impact of mentorship on personal and professional growth is explored.

- **Becoming a Mentor**
  - Offer to mentor others. Sharing your knowledge and experience not only helps others but also reinforces your own learning and growth.
  - Example: In "Mentor: The Kid & the CEO" by Tom Pace, the transformative power of mentorship is illustrated through a compelling narrative.

- **Coaching**
  - Engage in coaching relationships where you can receive or provide structured guidance aimed at achieving specific goals.

- Example: In "Coaching for Performance" by John Whitmore, the principles and techniques of effective coaching are outlined, showing how coaching can lead to enhanced performance and personal development.

Professional Associations and Groups

- **Joining Associations**
  - Join professional associations related to your field. These organisations often provide networking opportunities, resources, and professional development.
  - Example: In "The Professional Association Handbook" by Chris Butts, the benefits of joining professional associations are detailed, offering insights into how these groups can advance your career.

- **Active Participation**
  - Participate actively in association events, conferences, and forums. This visibility can lead to new connections and opportunities.
  - Example: In "The Conference Networking Guide" by Rob Lawless, strategies for maximizing networking opportunities at conferences and events are shared.

- **Leadership Roles**
  - Take on leadership roles within professional groups. This can enhance your reputation and expand your network.
  - Example: In "Leaders Eat Last" by Simon Sinek, the importance of leadership and its impact on professional relationships and organisational culture is discussed.

The Synergy Between Personal and Professional Relationships

The interplay between personal and professional relationships can create a synergistic effect that amplifies success. A supportive home environment can boost confidence and resilience, enabling individuals to tackle professional challenges with greater ease. Conversely, professional success can enhance personal relationships by providing financial stability and a sense of accomplishment.

Building Strong Personal Relationships

- **Open Communication**
  - Foster open and honest communication. Share your thoughts, feelings, and concerns with your loved ones.
  - Example: In "Men Are from Mars, Women Are from Venus" by John Gray, the importance of open communication in personal relationships is explored, providing strategies for improving communication between partners.

- **Empathy and Understanding**
  - Practice empathy by putting yourself in the other person's shoes. Understanding their perspective can strengthen your bond.
  - Example: In "To Kill a Mockingbird" by Harper Lee, Atticus Finch's empathetic approach to understanding others is a cornerstone of his character and teaches a valuable lesson in empathy.

- **Quality Time**
  - Spend quality time with your loved ones. It's not just about the quantity of time but the quality that matters.
  - Example: In "The 5 Love Languages" by Gary Chapman, the concept of quality time as a love language is discussed, highlighting its importance in building strong relationships.

- **Mutual Respect**
  - Respect each other's individuality and boundaries. Acknowledge and appreciate differences.
  - Example: In "The Seven Principles for Making Marriage Work" by John Gottman, mutual respect is identified as a key principle for successful relationships.

- **Support and Encouragement**
  - Be a pillar of support and encouragement. Celebrate each other's successes and provide comfort during tough times.
  - Example: In "The Road Less Traveled" by M. Scott Peck, the role of support and encouragement in personal development and relationships is explored.

The Importance of Building and Maintaining Solid Relationships

The significance of building and maintaining solid relationships cannot be overstated. Whether in our personal or professional lives, the connections we form with others play a critical role in our success and well-being.

Personal and Professional Connections

- **Personal Life:**
  - Emotional support from family, friends, and romantic partners
  - Motivation and sense of belonging
  - Enhanced mental and emotional resilience

- **Professional Life:**
  - Networking for professional growth and opportunities
  - Trust, respect, and shared goals
  - Collaboration and mutual value

Building Strong Networks

A strong network of relationships can provide security in times of hardship and open doors to new opportunities during prosperous times.

Professional Networks

- **Trust and Respect:**
  - Form the bedrock of professional relationships
  - Require sincerity, mutual value, and collaboration

- **Maintenance:**
  - Consistent communication
  - Active listening and support

- **Industry Events:**
  - Conferences, seminars, and networking gatherings
  - Engage with specialists, exchange ideas, stay updated on industry trends

- **Professional Organisations:**
  - Resources, mentorship opportunities, and networking platforms

- **Online Platforms:**
  - LinkedIn for fostering and nurturing professional connections
  - Engage with industry experts, participate in discussions, share valuable information

- **Mentorship:**
  - Seeking and offering guidance and expertise
  - Mentees bring fresh perspectives and enthusiasm

Personal Relationships

Our overall well-being and prosperity are deeply influenced by the strength of our personal relationships.

Key Elements of Healthy Relationships

- **Honest Communication:**
  - Address misunderstandings
  - Strengthen bonds of friendship

- **Trust:**
  - Built through consistency and dependability
  - Mutual respect for boundaries and individuality

- **Quality Time:**
  - Family gatherings, romantic evenings, casual hangouts with friends

- Create lasting memories and nurture bonds

- **Support and Encouragement:**
  - Vital for deepening connections
  - Foster a strong support system that bolsters resilience and emotional well-being

Adaptability and Growth

Adaptability is key in navigating the complexities of any relationship.

- **Compromise and Collaboration:**
  - Maintain a positive outlook
  - Address challenges and foster growth

- **Active Listening and Empathy:**
  - Find common ground
  - Adapt to changing circumstances and viewpoints

Final Thoughts

In both our personal and professional lives, effective communication and adaptability are essential for building and maintaining meaningful connections. By fostering trust, respect, and mutual support, we are better equipped to cultivate successful relationships that enrich our lives in multifaceted ways. Embracing relationship dynamics with an open heart and flexible mindset allows us to cultivate a supportive network that accompanies us through both trials and triumphs.

Ultimately, it is through these meaningful connections that we find fulfilment, resilience, and success in both our personal and professional endeavours. The man who effectively manages his own affairs while nurturing strong relationships flourishes in every aspect of life. By deliberately and conscientiously embracing and nurturing these connections, we pave the way for a fulfilling and empowering network that bolsters us through every challenge and celebrates every achievement.

8

Financial Planning for the Future

Economy is the third principle. The conservation of one's financial resources is merely the vestibule leading towards the more spacious chambers of true economy.

Financial planning is a cornerstone of personal and professional success, providing the stability and resources needed to achieve your goals. Effective financial management requires not only conserving resources but also making informed decisions to grow your wealth. This chapter explores the basics of financial literacy, strategies for planning financial stability, and principles of investing for a secure future.

Financial Planning

Financial planning is not just about saving money; it's about creating a comprehensive strategy to manage your finances in a way that aligns with your life goals. This involves understanding the intricacies of income, expenses, saving, investing, and risk management. A solid financial plan is dynamic and evolves with your life changes and economic conditions.

THE FOUNDATIONS OF FINANCIAL LITERACY

Understanding the Financial Ecosystem

The financial ecosystem consists of various elements such as banking, investments, insurance, and taxation. Each component plays a crucial role in shaping your financial health.

The Psychology of Money

Your financial decisions are deeply influenced by your attitudes towards money. Understanding your financial personality can help you make better financial decisions.

DETAILED BREAKDOWN OF FINANCIAL LITERACY

Income Management

Sources of Income

Income can come from multiple sources beyond a regular job, including dividends, interest, rental income, and business profits. Diversifying income streams can provide greater financial security.

Increasing Your Income

Strategies to increase your income include negotiating raises, acquiring new skills, switching careers, or starting a side business.

Expense Management

Fixed vs. Variable Expenses

Categorizing expenses into fixed (necessary, regular expenses) and variable (discretionary spending) helps in better budgeting.

Reducing Unnecessary Expenses

Implementing cost-saving measures, such as cutting down on subscriptions or dining out less frequently, can free up money for savings and investments.

Advanced Budgeting Techniques

Zero-Based Budgeting

Zero-based budgeting involves assigning every dollar a specific purpose, ensuring that income equals expenses plus savings and investments.

Envelope System

The envelope system allocates cash to different spending categories, helping you stick to your budget by avoiding overspending.

Saving Strategies

High-Yield Savings Accounts

High-yield savings accounts offer better interest rates compared to regular savings accounts, helping your money grow faster.

Automatic Transfers

Setting up automatic transfers to your savings account ensures consistent saving without the temptation to spend.

Comprehensive Debt Management

Debt Snowball vs. Debt Avalanche

The debt snowball method focuses on paying off the smallest debts first, while the debt avalanche method prioritises debts

Financial Planning for the Future

with the highest interest rates.

Debt Refinancing

Refinancing debt at a lower interest rate can save money over time and make debt repayment more manageable.

Understanding Credit

Building and Maintaining Good Credit

Steps to build good credit include paying bills on time, keeping credit card balances low, and not applying for too much credit at once.

Credit Report Monitoring

Regularly checking your credit report can help you catch errors and identify potential identity theft early.

Planning for Financial Stability

Setting SMART Financial Goals

SMART goals (Specific, Measurable, Achievable, Relevant, Time-bound) provide a clear roadmap for financial planning.

Developing a Financial Roadmap

A financial roadmap outlines the steps needed to achieve your financial goals, including budgeting, saving, investing, and debt management.

Retirement Planning in Detail

Different Types of Retirement Accounts

Understanding the differences between traditional and Roth

IRAs, 401(k)s, and other retirement accounts helps in making informed decisions.

Retirement Income Planning

Planning for a steady income stream during retirement involves understanding Social Security benefits, pension plans, and withdrawal strategies from retirement accounts.

Insurance and Risk Management

Types of Insurance

Different types of insurance, such as health, life, disability, and property insurance, play vital roles in protecting your financial future.

Choosing the Right Coverage

Evaluating your personal needs and risks helps in selecting the appropriate insurance coverage.

Tax Planning Strategies

Understanding Tax Brackets

Knowing your tax bracket helps in planning tax-efficient investments and deductions.

Utilizing Tax-Advantaged Accounts

Accounts like 529 plans for education savings or HSAs for medical expenses offer tax benefits that can enhance your financial plan.

Investing for Long-Term Growth

Types of Investment Vehicles

Exploring various investment vehicles such as stocks, bonds, mutual funds, ETFs, and real estate helps in building a diversified portfolio.

Active vs. Passive Investing

Active investing involves frequent trading to outperform the market, while passive investing focuses on long-term growth through index funds.

Advanced Investment Strategies

Alternative Investments

Investments in commodities, hedge funds, or private equity can provide diversification beyond traditional stocks and bonds.

Sustainable and Ethical Investing

Investing in companies that follow ethical practices or focus on sustainability can align your investments with your values.

Regular Review and Adjustment

Financial Health Check-Ups

Regularly assessing your financial health ensures that you stay on track with your goals and can make necessary adjustments.

Rebalancing Your Portfolio

Rebalancing involves adjusting your investments to maintain your desired asset allocation, especially after significant market movements.

Practical Financial Applications

Using Technology for Financial Management

Leveraging technology, such as financial planning software and mobile apps, can simplify managing your finances.

Financial Education Resources

Books, online courses, seminars, and financial advisors can provide valuable insights and guidance.

Professional Financial Planning

Working with Financial Advisors

A financial advisor can provide expert advice tailored to your personal situation, helping you navigate complex financial decisions.

Choosing the Right Financial Advisor

Selecting a financial advisor involves evaluating their credentials, experience, and fees to ensure they align with your needs.

Advanced Topics in Financial Planning

Estate Planning

Estate planning ensures that your assets are distributed according to your wishes and can include wills, trusts, and powers of attorney.

Philanthropic Planning

Incorporating charitable giving into your financial plan can provide tax benefits and support causes you care about.

Basics of Financial Literacy

1. Understanding Income and Expenses

Income Sources: Recognize all your sources of income, including salary, investments, side hustles, and passive income. Understanding your total income helps in budgeting and financial planning.

- o *Example*: John works a 9-to-5 job earning $50,000 annually, invests in dividend-paying stocks generating $2,000 per year, and runs a weekend photography business that brings in an additional $5,000.
- o *Important Point*: Diversifying income streams can provide financial security and reduce dependency on a single source.

Expense Tracking: Keep track of all your expenses, both fixed (rent, utilities) and variable (entertainment, dining out). This awareness is crucial for effective budgeting.

- o *Example*: Sarah uses a mobile app to log every purchase she makes, categorizing them into groceries, transportation, dining out, and subscriptions. This helps her see where she can cut back.
- o *Important Point*: Consistent expense tracking can reveal spending habits and highlight areas for potential savings.

2. Budgeting

Creating a Budget: Develop a budget that outlines your income and expenses. Allocate funds for necessities, savings, investments, and discretionary spending.

- *Example*: Mark allocates 50% of his income to essentials (rent, utilities), 20% to savings and investments, and 30% to discretionary spending (hobbies, dining out).
- *Important Point*: A well-structured budget ensures that all financial needs are met while still allowing for personal enjoyment.

Living Within Means: Ensure your expenses do not exceed your income. Aim to live below your means to save and invest more.

- *Example*: Emma earns $3,000 a month but only spends $2,500, putting the remaining $500 into a savings account and investments.
- *Important Point*: Living below your means can accelerate your financial growth and provide a cushion for unexpected expenses.

3. Saving

Emergency Fund: Establish an emergency fund that covers 3-6 months of living expenses. This fund provides a financial safety net in case of unexpected events.

- *Example*: Alex loses his job but is able to cover his expenses for five months using his emergency fund, giving him time to find a new job without financial stress.
- *Important Point*: An emergency fund can prevent financial ruin during crises and reduce the need for high-interest debt.

Short-term Savings: Save for short-term goals such as vacations, home renovations, or purchasing a new gadget. Regularly set aside money for these goals.

- *Example*: Rachel saves $200 monthly for a year to fund

her dream vacation, reaching her goal without going into debt.
- *Important Point*: Short-term savings help achieve personal goals without disrupting long-term financial plans.

4. Debt Management

Understanding Debt: Differentiate between good debt (investments in education, property) and bad debt (high-interest credit card debt). Manage and minimize bad debt.

- *Example*: Tom has a student loan with a low interest rate and a credit card debt with a high interest rate. He focuses on paying off the credit card debt first.
- *Important Point*: Prioritising high-interest debt reduction can save significant amounts of money over time.

Debt Repayment: Develop a strategy to pay off debts, prioritising high-interest debt first. Consider debt consolidation or refinancing for better terms.

- *Example*: Linda uses the debt avalanche method, paying off her highest interest debt first while making minimum payments on the rest.
- *Important Point*: Structured debt repayment plans can accelerate becoming debt-free and improve financial health.

5. Credit Management

Credit Score: Understand the importance of your credit score and how it affects your ability to obtain loans and favourable interest rates. Regularly check and maintain a good credit score.

- *Example*: Jason monitors his credit report annually and

disputes any errors, maintaining a high credit score that qualifies him for low-interest mortgage rates.
   - *Important Point*: A high credit score can save thousands of dollars in interest over the life of a loan.

Credit Utilization: Keep your credit utilization ratio low by managing credit card balances and paying off credit regularly.

   - *Example*: Maria ensures her credit card balances never exceed 30% of her credit limit, paying off her cards in full each month.
   - *Important Point*: Low credit utilization is a key factor in maintaining a good credit score and demonstrates responsible credit management.

Expanding Financial Literacy with Practical Applications

6. Expense Categorization

Fixed vs. Variable Expenses: Understand the difference between fixed expenses (non-negotiable costs like rent and utilities) and variable expenses (flexible costs like dining out and entertainment).

   - *Example*: Daniel distinguishes his fixed expenses of $1,200 per month from his variable expenses of $800, making adjustments to variable spending when needed.
   - *Important Point*: Knowing which expenses are fixed and which are variable helps in making necessary adjustments during financial planning.

Creating Spending Limits: Set spending limits for different categories to avoid overspending.

   - *Example*: Jessica sets a limit of $150 for monthly dining out and sticks to it, redirecting any extra money to her savings.

- o *Important Point*: Setting and adhering to spending limits can help avoid financial strain and encourage savings.

7. Financial Goal Setting

Long-Term vs. Short-Term Goals: Balance short-term financial desires with long-term objectives for a comprehensive financial plan.

- o *Example*: Lisa allocates funds towards a short-term goal of buying a laptop and a long-term goal of retirement savings.
- o *Important Point*: Balancing short-term and long-term goals ensures immediate needs are met without compromising future security.

8. Advanced Saving Techniques

High-Interest Savings Accounts: Utilize high-interest savings accounts to maximize the return on saved money.

- o *Example*: Kevin transfers his emergency fund to a high-yield savings account, earning higher interest compared to a regular account.
- o *Important Point*: High-interest accounts can significantly increase savings over time with minimal effort.

Certificate of Deposits (CDs): Invest in CDs for fixed, higher interest rates over specific terms.

- o *Example*: Nancy invests $10,000 in a 5-year CD, locking in a higher interest rate than a standard savings account.
- o *Important Point*: CDs offer a safe way to grow savings with guaranteed returns over a set period.

9. Building a Financial Safety Net

Insurance Policies: Secure various types of insurance (health, life, disability) to protect against unforeseen events.

- *Example*: Greg purchases life insurance to ensure his family is financially protected in case of his unexpected passing.
- *Important Point*: Insurance provides a crucial safety net that can prevent financial hardship in emergencies.

Long-Term Care Insurance: Consider long-term care insurance to cover potential future healthcare needs.

- *Example*: Emily buys long-term care insurance in her 40s to prepare for possible healthcare expenses in her later years.
- *Important Point*: Planning for long-term care can protect savings and provide peace of mind.

10. Exploring Investment Options

Diversified Portfolio: Create a diversified investment portfolio to spread risk across various asset classes.

- *Example*: Oliver invests in a mix of stocks, bonds, and real estate to balance risk and return.
- *Important Point*: Diversification helps mitigate risk and can lead to more stable long-term returns.

Understanding Market Trends: Stay informed about market trends to make educated investment decisions.

- *Example*: Laura follows financial news and market reports to adjust her investment strategy accordingly.
- *Important Point*: Knowledge of market trends allows for

more informed and potentially profitable investment choices.

Planning for Financial Stability

1. Setting Financial Goals

Short-term Goals: Identify short-term financial goals (1-3 years), such as paying off credit card debt, building an emergency fund, or saving for a vacation.

- o *Example*: Jamie sets a goal to pay off $3,000 in credit card debt within 18 months by allocating $167 from each paycheck towards the debt.
- o *Important Point*: Achieving short-term goals provides immediate rewards and builds momentum for tackling more substantial financial objectives.

Medium-term Goals: Define medium-term goals (3-5 years), such as saving for a down payment on a house, buying a car, or further education.

- o *Example*: Emma plans to save $20,000 over four years for a down payment on a house by setting aside $416 each month into a dedicated savings account.
- o *Important Point*: Medium-term goals require disciplined saving and often involve larger financial commitments that significantly impact future stability.

Long-term Goals: Establish long-term goals (5+ years), like retirement planning, children's education fund, or starting a business.

- o *Example*: Michael aims to accumulate $500,000 for retirement in 25 years by contributing $500 monthly to a retirement account with an average annual return of 6%.

- o *Important Point*: Long-term goals necessitate strategic planning and consistent contributions over an extended period to harness the power of compounding.

2. Developing a Financial Plan

Comprehensive Plan: Create a comprehensive financial plan that includes budgeting, saving, investing, and insurance. This plan should align with your financial goals.

- o *Example*: Sarah's financial plan includes a monthly budget, automated savings transfers, a diversified investment portfolio, and comprehensive insurance coverage.
- o *Important Point*: A well-rounded financial plan addresses all aspects of financial health, ensuring a balanced approach to achieving goals.

Review and Adjust: Regularly review your financial plan and adjust it based on life changes, market conditions, and progress towards goals.

- o *Example*: David reviews his financial plan quarterly, adjusting his investment allocations based on market performance and re-evaluating his goals as his family grows.
- o *Important Point*: Regular reviews keep the financial plan relevant and adaptable, allowing for proactive adjustments to stay on track.

3. Retirement Planning

Retirement Accounts: Contribute to retirement accounts like

401(k), IRA, or other pension plans. Take advantage of employer matches and tax benefits.

- o *Example*: Lisa maximizes her 401(k) contributions to receive the full employer match and invests in a Roth IRA for additional tax benefits.
- o *Important Point*: Leveraging retirement accounts and employer matches can significantly boost retirement savings and provide tax advantages.

Retirement Goals: Determine your retirement goals, including your desired lifestyle and estimated expenses. Plan your savings and investments accordingly.

- o *Example*: John calculates that he needs $1 million for retirement to maintain his current lifestyle and sets up a savings plan to reach this target.
- o *Important Point*: Clear retirement goals provide direction for savings and investment strategies, ensuring sufficient funds for desired retirement lifestyles.

4. Insurance

Health Insurance: Ensure you have adequate health insurance coverage to protect against medical expenses.

- o *Example*: Claire chooses a comprehensive health insurance plan that covers routine check-ups, emergency care, and specialist visits.
- o *Important Point*: Adequate health insurance protects against high medical costs and ensures access to necessary healthcare services.

Life Insurance: Consider life insurance to provide financial security for your dependents in case of your untimely death.

- *Example*: Peter purchases a term life insurance policy that covers 10 times his annual income to ensure his family is financially secure.
- *Important Point*: Life insurance provides a safety net for dependents, covering living expenses, education costs, and debt repayment in the policyholder's absence.

Property and Liability Insurance: Protect your assets with property and liability insurance. This includes home, auto, and personal liability coverage.

- *Example*: Maria insures her home and car and adds an umbrella liability policy for additional protection against potential lawsuits.
- *Important Point*: Property and liability insurance safeguard significant assets and provides financial protection against unforeseen incidents.

5. Tax Planning

Tax-efficient Investing: Invest in tax-advantaged accounts and consider tax implications of your investment strategies.

- *Example*: Greg invests in a 529 college savings plan for his children and uses a Roth IRA for retirement to benefit from tax-free growth and withdrawals.
- *Important Point*: Tax-efficient investments reduce tax liability and enhance overall returns, contributing to long-term financial growth.

Deductions and Credits: Maximize deductions and credits to reduce your taxable income. Stay informed about tax laws and changes.

- *Example*: Anna claims deductions for mortgage interest,

student loan interest, and charitable contributions, significantly lowering her taxable income.
- o *Important Point*: Taking full advantage of available deductions and credits minimizes tax burden and maximizes disposable income.

Expanding Financial Stability with Practical Applications

6. Emergency Planning

Creating an Emergency Fund: Establish an emergency fund to cover unexpected expenses such as medical emergencies, car repairs, or job loss.

- o *Example*: Nathan saves six months' worth of living expenses in a high-yield savings account, providing a buffer for unexpected financial setbacks.
- o *Important Point*: An emergency fund prevents financial disruption and reliance on high-interest debt during crises.

Income Protection: Consider disability insurance to replace a portion of your income if you are unable to work due to illness or injury.

- o *Example*: Laura purchases a long-term disability insurance policy that covers 60% of her salary, ensuring continued income if she becomes disabled.
- o *Important Point*: Disability insurance provides income continuity, protecting against the financial impact of loss of earning capacity.

7. Advanced Investment Strategies

Portfolio Diversification: Spread investments across different asset classes, sectors, and geographical regions to minimize risk.

- o *Example*: Ben diversifies his portfolio with stocks, bonds, real estate, and international investments, reducing exposure to any single market or asset class.
- o *Important Point*: Diversification reduces risk and can improve returns, providing a balanced approach to investment growth.

Regular Portfolio Rebalancing: Periodically adjust your investment portfolio to maintain your desired asset allocation.

- o *Example*: Chloe rebalances her portfolio annually, selling assets that have increased in value and buying those that have decreased to maintain her target allocation.
- o *Important Point*: Rebalancing maintains portfolio alignment with risk tolerance and investment goals, optimizing long-term performance.

8. Debt Reduction Techniques

Debt Snowball Method: Focus on paying off the smallest debt first while making minimum payments on others, then move to the next smallest debt.

- o *Example*: Steve pays off his $500 credit card balance first, then tackles his $1,500 personal loan, and finally his $5,000 student loan.
- o *Important Point*: The debt snowball method provides psychological wins and builds momentum for tackling larger debts.

Debt Avalanche Method: Prioritise paying off debts with the highest interest rates first, reducing the total interest paid over time.

- *Example*: Jane focuses on paying off her 20% interest credit card debt before addressing her 10% interest personal loan.
- *Important Point*: The debt avalanche method minimizes interest costs, accelerating overall debt repayment.

9. Enhancing Income Streams

Side Hustles: Explore additional income opportunities such as freelance work, part-time jobs, or starting a small business.

- *Example*: Ryan starts a weekend landscaping business, earning an extra $500 monthly, which he directs towards savings and investments.
- *Important Point*: Multiple income streams enhance financial security and accelerate goal achievement.

Passive Income: Invest in assets that generate passive income, such as rental properties, dividend-paying stocks, or peer-to-peer lending.

- *Example*: Olivia invests in rental properties, earning monthly rental income that supplements her salary and grows her wealth.
- *Important Point*: Passive income provides financial stability and can significantly boost overall wealth.

10. Financial Education and Professional Advice

Continuous Learning: Stay informed about personal finance through books, online courses, and financial news to make educated decisions.

- *Example*: Ethan regularly reads financial blogs and takes online courses to stay updated on investment strategies and tax laws.

- o *Important Point*: Ongoing education empowers informed financial decisions, adapting to changing circumstances and opportunities.

Seeking Professional Advice: Consult financial advisors for tailored advice and strategies to optimize financial planning.

- o *Example*: Rebecca works with a certified financial planner to create a customized investment strategy and retirement plan.
- o *Important Point*: Professional advice can provide expertise, objectivity, and personalized strategies, enhancing financial planning success.

By incorporating these additional detailed and practical examples, along with important points and further financial planning concepts, this section becomes an extensive guide for anyone seeking to enhance their financial stability and achieve long-term financial success.

Investing in Your Future

1. **Investment Principles**

    - o ***Diversification:*** Spread your investments across different asset classes (stocks, bonds, real estate) to reduce risk.
    - o ***Risk Tolerance:*** Understand your risk tolerance and invest accordingly. Younger investors may afford higher risk, while older investors might prefer conservative investments.
    - o ***Time Horizon:*** Align your investments with your time horizon. Short-term goals might require less volatile investments, while long-term goals can accommodate higher risk.

2. **Types of Investments**

    o   ***Stocks:*** Invest in individual stocks or stock mutual funds/ETFs for potential high returns. Understand the market and company performance before investing.

    o   ***Bonds:*** Bonds provide regular interest income and are generally less volatile than stocks. Consider government, municipal, or corporate bonds based on your risk tolerance.

    o   ***Real Estate:*** Real estate can provide rental income and capital appreciation. Evaluate the market and property value before investing.

    o   ***Mutual Funds and ETFs:*** Mutual funds and ETFs offer diversified exposure to various asset classes. They are managed by professionals and can be a good option for beginners.

3. **Retirement Accounts**

    o   ***401(k) and 403(b):*** Employer-sponsored retirement accounts with tax advantages. Maximize contributions to benefit from employer matches and tax deferrals.

    o   ***IRA (Traditional and Roth):*** Individual retirement accounts with tax benefits. Traditional IRAs offer tax-deferred growth, while Roth IRAs provide tax-free withdrawals.

    o   ***SEP IRA and SIMPLE IRA:*** Retirement plans for self-employed individuals and small business owners. They offer higher contribution limits and tax benefits.

4. **Investment Strategies**

    o   ***Dollar-Cost Averaging:*** Invest a fixed amount regularly, regardless of market conditions. This strategy reduces

the impact of market volatility.
- o ***Buy and Hold:*** Invest in high-quality assets and hold them long-term. This strategy capitalizes on the potential growth of the market over time.
- o ***Value Investing:*** Invest in undervalued stocks with strong fundamentals. This strategy focuses on long-term value rather than short-term gains.
- o ***Growth Investing:*** Invest in companies with high growth potential. This strategy aims for capital appreciation through rising stock prices.

5. **Monitoring and Rebalancing**

- o ***Regular Review:*** Regularly review your investment portfolio to ensure it aligns with your goals and risk tolerance. Adjust your investments based on performance and market conditions.
- o ***Rebalancing:*** Periodically rebalance your portfolio to maintain your desired asset allocation. This involves buying or selling assets to restore balance.

Practical Applications of Financial Planning

1. **In Personal Life**

- o ***Budgeting Tools:*** Use budgeting tools and apps like Mint, YNAB (You Need A Budget), or Personal Capital to manage your finances effectively.
- o ***Financial Education:*** Continuously educate yourself about personal finance through books, courses, and seminars. Knowledge is key to making informed decisions.

2. **In Professional Life**

   o *Employer Benefits*: Take full advantage of employer benefits, including retirement plans, health insurance, and employee stock purchase plans.

   o *Salary Negotiation*: Negotiate your salary and benefits to ensure you are compensated fairly. This can significantly impact your financial stability.

3. **In Business and Entrepreneurship**

   o *Business Budgeting*: Develop a comprehensive budget for your business, accounting for income, expenses, taxes, and investments.

   o *Investment in Business*: Reinvest profits into your business for growth and expansion. Consider financing options for larger investments.

4. **In Retirement Planning**

   o *Early Start*: Start retirement planning early to take advantage of compound interest. The earlier you start, the more you can save and grow your wealth.

   o *Retirement Lifestyle*: Plan for the lifestyle you want in retirement. Estimate expenses, including healthcare, travel, and leisure activities.

Advanced Investment Strategies

- *Hedge Funds and Private Equity*: Explore the world of hedge funds and private equity investments, including their potential benefits and risks.
- *Options and Futures*: Understand the basics of options and futures trading, and how these instruments can be used for hedging and speculative purposes.

Estate Planning

- ***Wills and Trusts:*** Learn about the importance of wills and trusts in estate planning, and how to set them up.
- **Estate Taxes**: Understand the implications of estate taxes and strategies to minimize their impact.

Philanthropy and Charitable Giving

- ***Donor-Advised Funds:*** Explore the benefits of donor-advised funds for charitable giving.
- ***Charitable Trusts:*** Learn how to establish charitable trusts and their benefits for long-term philanthropic goals.

Global Financial Planning

- ***Investing Internationally:*** Understand the benefits and risks of investing in foreign markets.
- ***Currency Risk Management***: Learn strategies to manage currency risk in international investments.

Behavioural Finance

- ***Investor Psychology:*** Explore how emotions and psychological biases can impact financial decisions.
- ***Overcoming Biases:*** Learn strategies to overcome common psychological biases in investing.

Technological Impact on Finance

- ***Fintech Innovations:*** Discover how fintech innovations are transforming personal finance and investment management.
- ***Blockchain and Cryptocurrencies:*** Understand the basics of blockchain technology and cryptocurrencies, and their potential impact on the financial industry.

Final Thoughts

Financial planning is a critical component of long-term success and security. By understanding the basics of financial literacy, developing a comprehensive financial plan, and making informed investment decisions, you can achieve financial stability and growth. Remember, the conservation of financial resources is just the beginning. True economy involves strategic planning, disciplined saving, and wise investing to build a secure and prosperous future. Embrace these principles, and you will be well-equipped to navigate the financial landscape and achieve your goals.

PART TWO

WHOLESOMENESS AND WELLNESS CARE

The destiny of happiness and tragedy lies within the hands of man. Astonishingly, it is he who holds the key to his own joy and sorrow. These emotions do not descend upon him from the external world, but rather, reside within his very being. Nurturing one's health and well-being is imperative for leading a fulfilling and purposeful life. Our overall contentment, effectiveness, and accomplishments are profoundly influenced by the state of our physical and mental well-being. By taking proactive measures to safeguard our health, we can create and maintain an environment that fosters well-being and productivity. In the following chapter, we will explore the intricate connection between health and productivity, uncover the essentials of physical wellness, and discover strategies for nurturing mental well-being. Human beings are the master artisans of their own happiness and suffering. Indeed, man is both the creator and guardian of his own inner joy and pain. These sentiments do not descend from the skies; rather, they spring from the depths of our hearts. When it comes to leading a life of vigor and significance, health and well-being form the bedrock. Our physical and emotional states impact every aspect of our lives, from the daily joy we experience to the long-term achievements we attain. By taking charge of our health and adopting preventive measures, we have the power to cultivate a sanctuary of well-being that will fuel our productivity and success. In the riveting chapters to come, we will explore the intricate interplay between health and productivity, unearth the secrets of physical vitality, and unlock the principles of mental fortitude.

9

Health and Wellness

Participating in and promoting community wellness projects and advocating for public health policies are important ways to make a positive impact.

Individual health and wellness can significantly contribute to the well-being of the community and the world additionally, supporting global health campaigns and adopting sustainable behaviours that benefit human health and the environment can contribute to a healthier world. Encouraging businesses and organisations to implement health and wellness policies that benefit employees and the community is crucial for social responsibility. This may include corporate wellness programs that provide mental health support, gym memberships, and healthy food options. Looking ahead, emerging trends in health and wellness, such as telehealth expansion, wearable technology for real-time health data, personalized medicine based on genetic profiles, and increased focus on mental health, are expected to shape the future of productivity and happiness.

The Philosophy of Wellness

- **Ancient Wisdom:** Exploring how different cultures

throughout history have understood and promoted the idea that happiness and misery are shaped by internal conditions. For example, the teachings of Buddha on the Four Noble Truths and the Eightfold Path, and Stoic philosophy emphasizing control over one's perceptions and reactions.

- **Self-Realization:** The journey of understanding oneself and one's internal landscape. Discuss practices such as journaling, self-reflection, and meditation as tools for gaining insight into one's internal conditions.

Modern Perspectives

- **Scientific Validation:** How modern research supports ancient beliefs about the mind-body connection. Studies showing the impact of positive thinking on physical health, such as the placebo effect, and the role of stress in chronic diseases.
- **Mind-Body Techniques:** Introduction of techniques such as biofeedback, mindfulness-based stress reduction (MBSR), and cognitive-behavioural therapy (CBT) that are used to improve mental and physical health.

Personal Responsibility

- **Empowerment Through Knowledge:** Educating individuals about their own health and wellness, including understanding medical conditions, treatment options, and lifestyle changes.
- **Behavioral Change Models:** The Stages of Change model (Precontemplation, Contemplation, Preparation, Action, Maintenance) and how individuals can use this framework to make lasting changes in their health behaviours.

THE CONNECTION BETWEEN HEALTH AND PRODUCTIVITY

Physical Health and Productivity

- **Workplace Wellness Programs:** Case studies of companies that have implemented successful wellness programs and the measurable impact on employee productivity and job satisfaction.
- **Community Health Initiatives:** Examples of community health programs that have improved public health and local productivity, such as Blue Zones projects which promote longevity and well-being.

Mental Health and Productivity

- **Corporate Mental Health Initiatives:** Examination of companies that prioritise mental health, providing resources such as counselling services, mental health days, and stress management workshops.
- **Educational Systems:** How schools and universities are incorporating mental health education and support services to improve student performance and well-being.

HOLISTIC HEALTH APPROACH

Integrating Physical and Mental Health

- **Case Studies:** Real-world examples of individuals who have successfully integrated physical and mental health practices to achieve balance and optimal productivity.
- Wellness Retreats: Analysis of wellness retreats and their impact on holistic health, featuring retreats like those at the Kripalu Center for Yoga & Health and Canyon Ranch.

Preventive Health Measures

- **Public Health Campaigns:** Discussion of successful public health campaigns that focus on prevention, such as anti-smoking initiatives and vaccination drives.
- **Technological Innovations:** The role of wearable technology and health apps in promoting preventive health measures and tracking personal health metrics.

PHYSICAL WELLNESS: EXERCISE, DIET, SLEEP

Exercise

- **Exercise Science:** In-depth exploration of the science behind different types of exercise, such as high-intensity interval training (HIIT), aerobic exercise, and resistance training.
- **Success Stories:** Profiles of individuals who have transformed their lives through exercise, including their routines and the physical and mental benefits they experienced.

Diet

- **Nutritional Studies:** Analysis of landmark nutritional studies, such as the Mediterranean Diet and its long-term health benefits.
- **Dietary Challenges:** Exploration of common dietary challenges, such as food deserts and socioeconomic factors affecting access to healthy food.

Sleep

- **Sleep Research:** Summarizing key findings from sleep research, including the impact of sleep on memory consolidation, emotional regulation, and immune function.
- **Sleep Disorders:** Overview of common sleep disorders like

insomnia and sleep apnea, including their impact on health and strategies for management.

MENTAL WELLNESS: STRESS MANAGEMENT, MINDFULNESS

Advanced Stress Management Techniques

- **Innovative Therapies:** Examination of cutting-edge therapies for stress management, such as virtual reality therapy and transcranial magnetic stimulation (TMS).
- **Global Practices:** How different cultures manage stress, from Scandinavian hygge to Japanese forest bathing (shinrin-yoku).

Mindfulness in Everyday Life

- **Practical Applications:** Detailed guides on incorporating mindfulness into daily routines, including mindful eating, mindful walking, and mindful communication.
- **Mindfulness in Education:** Programs like MindUP and Mindful Schools that teach mindfulness to children and their impact on student behaviour and academic performance.

EMOTIONAL REGULATION

Emotional Awareness and Intelligence

- **Emotional Intelligence (EQ):** The importance of EQ in personal and professional life, including strategies to enhance EQ, such as empathy training and emotional regulation techniques.
- **Therapeutic Practices:** Exploration of various therapeutic practices for emotional regulation, including dialectical behaviour therapy (DBT) and emotion-focused therapy (EFT).

SELF-CARE

Comprehensive Self-Care Plans

- **Holistic Approaches:** Developing personalized self-care plans that address physical, mental, emotional, and spiritual needs.
- **Self-Care Movements:** Exploration of the self-care movement, its origins, and its growing importance in contemporary culture.

Preventive Health Measures

- **Innovative Preventive Measures:** How advances in genetic testing and personalized medicine are revolutionizing preventive health care.
- **Preventive Health Campaigns:** Successful global health campaigns, such as those for HIV/AIDS prevention and anti-obesity efforts.

Technology and Self-Care

- **Health Tech:** The role of modern technology in promoting health and wellness, including fitness trackers, mental health apps, and telemedicine.

The Connection Between Health and Productivity

1. **Physical Health and Productivity**
    - **Energy Levels:** Good physical health boosts energy levels, enabling you to maintain focus and productivity throughout the day. Regular exercise and a balanced diet are key contributors.
    - **Reduced Absenteeism:** Healthy individuals are less

likely to suffer from illnesses that cause absenteeism, leading to more consistent performance at work or in personal endeavours.
- **Enhanced Cognitive Function:** Physical activity increases blood flow to the brain, enhancing cognitive functions such as memory, concentration, and problem-solving skills.
- Impact on Daily Routines: Detailed analysis of how physical health impacts daily routines and long-term achievements.
- Case Studies: Real-life examples of individuals and organisations that have successfully integrated physical health into their productivity strategies.
- Advanced Nutrition: Exploring the role of specific nutrients and dietary patterns in enhancing physical health and energy levels.
-

2. **Mental Health and Productivity**

    - **Focus and Clarity:** Mental well-being enhances focus and clarity, allowing you to tackle tasks with greater efficiency. Stress and anxiety can cloud judgement and reduce productivity.
    - **Emotional Stability:** Emotional stability contributes to better decision-making and interpersonal interactions. A balanced mental state promotes a positive work environment and collaboration.
    - **Motivation and Drive:** Mental wellness boosts motivation and drive, helping you stay committed to your goals. It fosters a positive attitude towards challenges and setbacks.
    - In-depth Analysis: Exploring the neurological and

psychological mechanisms linking mental health to productivity.
- Long-term Effects: How sustained mental health issues can affect career longevity and personal achievements.
- Innovative Solutions: New approaches to maintaining mental health in high-stress environments, such as tech companies or financial sectors.

3. **Holistic Health Approach**

    - **Integration of Physical and Mental Health:** Physical and mental health are interconnected. A holistic approach to wellness involves nurturing both aspects to achieve optimal productivity and happiness.
    - **Preventive Health Measures:** Regular health check-ups, a balanced lifestyle, and preventive measures reduce the risk of chronic diseases and enhance long-term well-being.
    - **Synergistic Effects:** Detailed examination of how physical and mental health interact and support each other.
    - **Cultural Practices:** How different cultures approach holistic health and what can be learned from them.

Physical Wellness: Exercise, Diet, Sleep

1. **Exercise**

    - **Types of Exercise:** Incorporate a variety of exercises into your routine, including cardiovascular activities (running, swimming), strength training (weight lifting, resistance bands), and flexibility exercises (yoga, stretching).

- **Benefits of Exercise:** Regular exercise improves cardiovascular health, strengthens muscles, enhances flexibility, and boosts immune function. It also releases endorphins, which elevate mood and reduce stress.
- **Exercise Routine:** Aim for at least 150 minutes of moderate-intensity aerobic activity or 75 minutes of vigorous-intensity activity per week, combined with muscle-strengthening activities on two or more days per week.
- Integrative Exercise Plans: Creating personalized exercise plans that adapt to various life stages and health conditions.
- Superfoods and Diet Trends: Evaluating the science behind popular diet trends and their actual benefits.
- Sleep Science: Latest research on sleep cycles, the impact of sleep deprivation, and advanced sleep optimization techniques.
-

2. **Diet**

- **Balanced Diet:** Consume a balanced diet rich in fruits, vegetables, whole grains, lean proteins, and healthy fats. Proper nutrition fuels your body and supports overall health.
- **Hydration:** Stay hydrated by drinking plenty of water throughout the day. Proper hydration is essential for maintaining bodily functions and energy levels.
- **Mindful Eating:** Practice mindful eating by paying attention to hunger and fullness cues, savouring your food, and avoiding distractions while eating. This promotes better digestion and prevents overeating.

3. Sleep

- **Importance of Sleep:** Adequate sleep is crucial for physical and mental health. It allows the body to repair and regenerate, supports cognitive function, and regulates mood.
- **Sleep Hygiene:** Maintain good sleep hygiene by establishing a regular sleep schedule, creating a restful environment, and avoiding stimulants (caffeine, electronic devices) before bedtime.
- **Sleep Duration:** Aim for 7-9 hours of quality sleep per night. Consistent sleep patterns improve overall health and productivity.

Mental Wellness: Stress Management, Mindfulness

1. Stress Management

- **Identifying Stressors:** Identify the sources of stress in your life, whether they are related to work, relationships, or personal challenges. Understanding your stressors is the first step in managing them.
- **Stress Reduction Techniques:** Implement stress reduction techniques such as deep breathing exercises, progressive muscle relaxation, and visualization. These practices help calm the mind and body.
- **Time Management:** Effective time management reduces stress by helping you prioritise tasks, set realistic goals, and avoid procrastination. Break tasks into manageable steps and allocate time for relaxation.
- Advanced Stress Management Techniques: Including biofeedback, neurofeedback, and other high-tech solutions.

- Mindfulness in Everyday Life: Practical applications of mindfulness in personal and professional settings, with step-by-step guides.
- Emotional Intelligence: Developing emotional intelligence and its importance in managing stress and relationships.

2. Mindfulness

- **Mindfulness Practices:** Engage in mindfulness practices such as meditation, yoga, and tai chi. These activities promote present-moment awareness and reduce stress.
- **Mindful Breathing:** Practice mindful breathing by focusing on your breath, inhaling deeply through the nose, and exhaling slowly through the mouth. This simple practice can be done anytime to reduce anxiety.
- **Gratitude Practice:** Cultivate gratitude by regularly reflecting on the positive aspects of your life. Keeping a gratitude journal can enhance mental well-being and foster a positive outlook.

3. Emotional Regulation

- **Emotional Awareness:** Develop emotional awareness by recognizing and acknowledging your emotions. Understanding your emotional triggers helps in managing reactions and responses.
- **Healthy Expression:** Express your emotions healthily through talking, writing, or creative activities. Bottling up emotions can lead to increased stress and mental health issues.
- **Support Systems:** Build a strong support system of friends, family, and mental health professionals. Sharing

your feelings and seeking support can alleviate emotional burdens.
- o Advanced Emotional Awareness: Techniques to deepen emotional self-awareness and improve emotional regulation.
- o Therapeutic Approaches: Overview of various therapeutic approaches to emotional health, including cognitive-behavioural therapy, psychodynamic therapy, and alternative therapies like art and music therapy.
- o

4. **Self-Care**

   - o **Self-Care Activities:** Engage in self-care activities that nourish your body, mind, and spirit. This can include hobbies, relaxation techniques, and spending time in nature.
   - o **Setting Boundaries:** Set healthy boundaries to protect your time and energy. Learn to say no to commitments that overwhelm you and prioritise activities that enhance your well-being.
   - o **Regular Breaks:** Take regular breaks throughout the day to rest and recharge. Short breaks can improve focus and productivity.
   - o Preventive Health Measures: Advanced preventive health measures, including genetic testing and personalized medicine.
   - o Technology and Self-Care: Using apps and wearable technology to track and enhance self-care routines.

Practical Applications of Health and Wellness

1. In Personal Life

- **Life Stages:** How health and wellness practices should evolve through different life stages, from adolescence to old age.
- **Chronic Illness Management:** Strategies for managing chronic illnesses while maintaining productivity and quality of life.
- **Daily Routine:** Establish a daily routine that includes exercise, healthy meals, and sufficient sleep. Consistency in these habits promotes long-term health.
- **Healthy Relationships:** Foster healthy relationships by communicating openly, spending quality time with loved ones, and offering support and encouragement.
- **Personal Goals:** Set personal health goals, such as improving fitness levels, losing weight, or managing stress. Track your progress and celebrate achievements.

2. In Professional Life

- **Remote Work Wellness:** Addressing the unique health challenges and opportunities presented by remote work.
- **Corporate Wellness Programs:** Detailed exploration of the most successful corporate wellness programs globally.
- **Work-Life Balance:** Strive for a healthy work-life balance by setting boundaries between work and personal life. Allocate time for relaxation and leisure activities.
- **Ergonomics:** Create an ergonomic workspace that supports physical health. Use ergonomic furniture, take regular breaks, and practice good posture.
- **Wellness Programs:** Participate in workplace wellness

programs that promote physical and mental health. These programs can include fitness challenges, mental health resources, and wellness workshops.

3. **In Business and Entrepreneurship**

    o **Health-Oriented Business Models:** Examples of businesses built around promoting health and wellness.
    o **Leadership and Health:** How leaders can model healthy behaviours and create a culture of wellness in their organisations.
    o **Healthy Work Environment:** Foster a healthy work environment by promoting physical activity, providing healthy snacks, and encouraging regular breaks.
    o **Stress Management Resources:** Offer stress management resources such as employee assistance programs, counselling services, and stress reduction workshops.
    o **Leadership by Example:** Lead by example by prioritising your health and wellness. Encourage your team to do the same and create a culture of well-being.

4. **In Education**

    o **Comprehensive Wellness Education:** Developing curriculums that, mental, and emotional health education.
    o **Teacher and Student Wellness Programs:** Successful case studies of wellness programs in schools and universities.
    o **Student Wellness:** Promote student wellness by incorporating physical activity, healthy eating, and mental health education into the curriculum.
    o **Teacher Well-being:** Support teacher well-being by providing resources for stress management, professional

development, and work-life balance.
- o **Wellness Initiatives:** Implement school-wide wellness initiatives that promote a healthy and supportive learning environment.

Developing a long-term perspective involves setting health and wellness goals and devising strategies to achieve and maintain them. Continuous learning and adaptation should be integral to your health journey, which can involve participating in wellness seminars, enrolling in nutrition classes, and staying updated with the latest health research developments. Regularly reassessing and modifying your health and wellness plans is crucial. Quarterly health check-ins can help you review your goals, identify obstacles, and celebrate progress. Keeping detailed personal health records that encompass medical history, dietary habits, exercise routines, and mental well-being is essential for making informed decisions about your future health and communicating effectively with healthcare professionals. Building a strong support system that includes friends, family, healthcare providers, and wellness coaches is imperative. Regular engagement with these networks can provide motivation, advice, and accountability. Lastly, the growing popularity of virtual wellness programs and the application of gamification in health apps to motivate and engage users in their wellness journeys are further developments to be aware of.

10

Leveraging Technology for Productivity

All things whether visible or invisible are subservient to and fall within the scope of this infinite and eternal law of causation.

The impact of technology on productivity cannot be overstated. By understanding the law of causation—how every action has a corresponding effect—we can harness technology to enhance our productivity, efficiency, and overall success. This chapter explores the role of technology in modern productivity, introduces tools and apps that can enhance productivity, and discusses strategies for balancing technology use to avoid burnout and distraction.

The Role of Technology in Modern Productivity

1. **Automation and Efficiency**

    o ***Automating Tasks:*** Technology enables the automation of repetitive and mundane tasks, freeing up time for more strategic and creative activities. Automation tools like IFTTT (If This Then That) and Zapier streamline workflows by connecting different apps and automating tasks.

- ***Increased Efficiency:*** Technology enhances efficiency by providing quick access to information, facilitating communication, and streamlining processes. It allows for the execution of complex tasks with greater speed and accuracy.

2. **Communication and Collaboration**

   - ***Instant Communication:*** Tools like Slack, Microsoft Teams, and Zoom enable instant communication, making it easier to collaborate with colleagues, regardless of geographical location. These platforms support real-time messaging, video conferencing, and file sharing.
   - ***Collaborative Platforms:*** Collaborative platforms like Google Workspace and Microsoft Office 365 allow multiple users to work on documents, spreadsheets, and presentations simultaneously. This fosters teamwork and reduces the time spent on revisions and email exchanges.

3. **Project Management**

   - ***Organised Workflow:*** Project management tools like Trello, Asana, and Monday.com help organise tasks, set deadlines, and track progress. These tools provide a visual overview of projects, ensuring that all team members are aligned and focused on their responsibilities.
   - ***Task Prioritisation:*** These platforms enable the prioritisation of tasks based on urgency and importance, helping teams focus on high-impact activities and meet deadlines efficiently.

4. **Data Analysis and Decision Making**

   - ***Data-Driven Insights:*** Technology provides access to powerful data analytics tools like Tableau, Power BI, and

Google Analytics. These tools help analyse large datasets, uncover patterns, and generate actionable insights for informed decision-making.

- o *Predictive Analytics:* Advanced technologies like machine learning and artificial intelligence (AI) enable predictive analytics, helping businesses anticipate trends, optimize operations, and make strategic decisions.

5. **Remote Work and Flexibility**

- o *Remote Work Tools:* Technologies such as VPNs, cloud storage, and remote desktop applications facilitate remote work, providing employees with the flexibility to work from anywhere. This adaptability has become especially crucial in the wake of global events like the COVID-19 pandemic.
- o *Work-Life Balance:* The flexibility offered by remote work tools contributes to a better work-life balance, as employees can manage their schedules more effectively and reduce commuting time.

Tools and Apps to Enhance Productivity

1. **Task Management and To-Do Lists**

- o *Microsoft To Do:* An intuitive app for creating to-do lists, setting reminders, and organising tasks. It integrates with Microsoft Office 365, making it ideal for users in the Microsoft ecosystem.

2. **Note-Taking and Documentation**

- o *Evernote:* A versatile note-taking app that allows you to capture, organise, and share notes. Evernote supports text, images, audio, and web clippings, making it a comprehensive tool for documentation.

- o *OneNote*: A digital notebook that integrates with Microsoft Office, allowing you to create, organise, and collaborate on notes. OneNote's flexibility and integration make it a valuable tool for both personal and professional use.

3. **File Storage and Sharing**

   - o *Google Drive*: A cloud storage service that allows you to store, share, and collaborate on files. Google Drive integrates with Google Workspace apps like Docs, Sheets, and Slides.
   - o *Dropbox*: A cloud storage platform that supports file syncing, sharing, and collaboration. Dropbox offers seamless integration with various tools and services.

Balancing Technology Use

1. **Avoiding Digital Overload**

   - o *Digital Detox:* Regularly disconnect from digital devices to recharge and focus on offline activities. Set aside time each day or week for a digital detox to reduce screen fatigue.
   - o *Screen Time Management*: Use screen time management tools to monitor and limit your usage of digital devices. Apps like Apple's Screen Time and Google's Digital Wellbeing help track and manage screen time.

2. **Setting Boundaries**

   - o *Work-Life Boundaries:* Establish clear boundaries between work and personal life. Set specific work hours

and avoid checking work emails or messages outside those hours.
- ○ ***Notification Management:*** Manage notifications to minimize distractions. Disable non-essential notifications and use do-not-disturb modes during focused work periods.

3. **Mindful Technology Use**

   - ○ ***Intentional Usage:*** Be intentional about how and when you use technology. Focus on using tools and apps that enhance productivity rather than those that distract.
   - ○ ***Purposeful Breaks:*** Take regular breaks to rest your eyes and mind. Use these breaks to engage in physical activity, stretch, or spend time outdoors.

4. **Healthy Digital Habits**

   - ○ ***Ergonomics:*** Ensure your workspace is ergonomically designed to prevent physical strain. Use ergonomic chairs, keyboards, and monitors to maintain good posture.
   - ○ ***Blue Light Management:*** Reduce exposure to blue light from screens, especially before bedtime. Use blue light filters or glasses to protect your eyes and improve sleep quality.

5. **Continuous Learning and Adaptation**

   - ○ ***Stay Updated:*** Stay informed about the latest technology trends and updates. Continuous learning helps you leverage new tools and features effectively.
   - ○ ***Adaptation:*** Be open to adapting your technology use based on changing needs and preferences. Regularly assess your tools and workflows to ensure they remain effective.

Final Thoughts: The Techie Tango to Turbocharge Your Productivity

Alright folks, let's talk tech – not the boring, *"did-you-turn-it-off-and-on"* kind, but the shiny, life-altering, productivity-boosting sort! Imagine your life as a chaotic dance floor, and technology is that groovy partner who always knows the right moves to make you look like a pro. Buckle up for a hilarious yet enlightening deep dive into how to twirl and whirl your way to peak productivity with the help of our digital pals.

Understanding the Digital Dance Floor

First things first, let's recognize that technology isn't just a fancy new gadget in the corner; it's the DJ spinning the tunes of efficiency and success. By syncing with this rhythm, you can transform your workspace into a harmonious symphony of collaboration and well-being. But how do we do this without stepping on our own toes? Let's break it down.

Daily Dance Practice: Practical Strategies

From personal life to professional settings, here's how you can keep your productivity dance smooth and steady:

- **Personal Chores**: Use Todoist to keep track of everything from grocery shopping to personal projects. It's like having a dance instructor keeping you on beat.
- **Professional Growth**: Platforms like Coursera and LinkedIn Learning are your dance classes, helping you master new skills and stay ahead.
- **Business Management**: Salesforce and HubSpot are like the backstage crew, ensuring everything runs smoothly while you take the spotlight.
- **Educational Engagement**: Kahoot! and Moodle turn

learning into a fun dance party, making it interactive and engaging.

Final Take

In this ever-evolving digital dance hall, the right steps with technology can lead to a show-stopping performance of productivity and success. By understanding the crucial role technology plays, picking the right tools, and balancing their use, you can choreograph a life of efficiency and well-being. Every move you make with technology can lead to better outcomes, so embrace these strategies and let technology be your partner in the dance of life. Now, go out there and dance like nobody's watching – but with a perfectly organised to-do list in your pocket!

11

Overcoming Obstacles and Resilience

He who would make his own the wisdom which is inherent in those principles must not merely have them on his lips; they must be established in his heart.

Overcoming obstacles and developing resilience are essential for achieving long-term success and fulfilment. True wisdom and resilience come from deeply ingraining principles in our hearts, not just understanding them intellectually. This chapter explores common obstacles to success, strategies for developing resilience, and inspiring stories of individuals who have demonstrated extraordinary resilience and perseverance.

Common Obstacles to Success

1. **Fear of Failure**
    - *Paralysis by Fear:* The fear of failing can prevent individuals from taking risks and pursuing their goals. This fear can lead to inaction and missed opportunities.
    - *Negative Self-Talk:* Negative self-talk and doubt can undermine confidence and create a self-fulfilling prophecy of failure.

2. Lack of Motivation

- ***Procrastination:*** A lack of motivation often leads to procrastination, where tasks are delayed and deadlines are missed. This can result in poor performance and missed opportunities.
- ***Burnout:*** Persistent stress and overworking can lead to burnout, characterised by exhaustion, cynicism, and a lack of accomplishment.

3. Limited Resources

- ***Financial Constraints:*** Insufficient financial resources can hinder the ability to invest in education, training, or business ventures.
- ***Lack of Access:*** Limited access to information, mentorship, and networking opportunities can impede personal and professional growth.

4. Negative Influences

- ***Toxic Relationships:*** Relationships with negative or toxic individuals can drain energy, undermine confidence, and create a hostile environment.
- ***Unsupportive Environment:*** An unsupportive work or home environment can stifle creativity, productivity, and growth.

5. Self-Doubt and Low Self-Esteem

- ***Imposter Syndrome:*** Feelings of inadequacy and the fear of being exposed as a fraud can prevent individuals from pursuing opportunities and achieving their potential.
- ***Negative Comparisons:*** Constantly comparing oneself

to others can lead to feelings of inferiority and self-doubt.

6. **Physical and Mental Health Challenges**

    o *Chronic Illness:* Physical health issues can limit the ability to work, study, or engage in activities that contribute to success.

    o *Mental Health Issues:* Mental health challenges such as anxiety, depression, and stress can impede focus, motivation, and overall well-being.

Developing Resilience

1. **Embracing a Growth Mindset**

    o *Learning from Failure:* View failures as opportunities to learn and grow. Embrace the belief that abilities and intelligence can be developed through effort and perseverance.

    o *Positive Outlook:* Maintain a positive outlook and focus on possibilities rather than limitations. Cultivate optimism and a can-do attitude.

2. **Building Emotional Intelligence**

    o *Self-Awareness:* Develop self-awareness by recognizing and understanding your emotions. This awareness helps in managing reactions and responses.

    o *Empathy:* Cultivate empathy to understand and connect with others. Empathy fosters strong relationships and emotional support.

3. **Strengthening Support Networks**

    o *Social Connections:* Build and maintain strong social

connections with friends, family, and colleagues. A supportive network provides emotional support and practical assistance.

o **Seeking Mentorship:** Seek guidance from mentors who can offer insights, advice, and encouragement. Mentorship provides valuable perspective and support.

4. **Practising Self-Care**

   o **Physical Health:** Prioritise physical health through regular exercise, a balanced diet, and adequate sleep. Physical well-being supports mental and emotional resilience.

   o **Mental Health:** Engage in activities that promote mental health, such as mindfulness, meditation, and hobbies. Taking time for self-care reduces stress and enhances well-being.

5. **Setting Realistic Goals**

   o **SMART Goals:** Set Specific, Measurable, Achievable, Relevant, and Time-bound (SMART) goals. Break down larger goals into smaller, manageable steps.

   o **Progress Tracking:** Track progress and celebrate achievements, no matter how small. Recognizing progress boosts motivation and confidence.

6. **Developing Coping Strategies**

   o **Stress Management:** Implement stress management techniques such as deep breathing, progressive muscle relaxation, and visualization. These practices help calm the mind and body.

   o **Problem-Solving Skills:** Enhance problem-solving skills by analysing situations, identifying solutions, and taking decisive action. Effective problem-solving builds confidence and resilience.

7. **Fostering Adaptability**

       o   *Flexibility:* Stay flexible and open to change. Adaptability helps in navigating new challenges and opportunities.
       o   *Continuous Learning:* Commit to lifelong learning and skill development. Staying informed and acquiring new skills enhances resilience and adaptability.

8. **Maintaining Perspective**

       o   *Long-Term View:* Maintain a long-term perspective and focus on overall progress rather than short-term setbacks. This helps in staying motivated and resilient.
       o   *Gratitude Practice:* Cultivate gratitude by regularly reflecting on positive aspects of life. Keeping a gratitude journal enhances mental well-being and fosters a positive outlook.

PART THREE

LIFELONG LEARNING AND LEGACY

Lifelong learning and skill development are not mere buzzwords; they are the bedrock of personal and professional success.

The journey of continuous learning isn't just about acquiring knowledge—it's about evolving as a person, adapting to the ever-changing world, and leaving a lasting legacy. Let's delve deep into this odyssey, exploring strategies, theories, real-life examples, and stories that illustrate the profound impact of lifelong learning. *In a world where change is the only constant, adaptability becomes a crucial skill.* For instance, consider the story of Mary Barra, the CEO of General Motors, who began her career as a co-op student at GM and continuously learned and adapted, eventually leading the company through significant transformations in the automotive industry. Barra's story exemplifies how embracing lifelong learning can lead to unparalleled career success. Charles Darwin's theory of natural selection underscores the importance of adaptability. Just as species evolve to survive in their environments, individuals must continuously learn and adapt to thrive in their personal and professional lives. This theory is not just about survival but about thriving and succeeding in a competitive world. Imagine you're setting off on a long journey—you need a map, a destination, and a plan. Similarly, a learning plan acts as your roadmap to success. Identify skills that align with your career goals and personal interests. For example, if you're a software developer, learning the latest programming languages and frameworks keeps you relevant in the industry. *The SMART framework—Specific, Measurable, Achievable, Relevant, and Time-bound—can help in setting and achieving learning goals.* For instance, John, an accountant, decided to enhance his skills in data analytics. By setting a SMART goal to complete a certified data analytics course within six months, John was able to systematically improve his skills and advance his career. Technology is a treasure trove for lifelong learners. Online platforms like Coursera, edX, and Udemy offer a plethora of courses across various disciplines. Consider the story of Priya, a marketing professional who used LinkedIn Learning to master digital marketing strategies, which not only expanded her skill set but also opened up new career opportunities. Albert Bandura's social learning theory emphasizes the importance of observing and modelling the behaviours, attitudes, and emotional reactions of others. In the digital age, social learning can occur through online communities, webinars, and virtual study groups, providing a rich, collaborative learning experience. *Continuous learning keeps the mind agile and engaged.* Take the example of Leonardo da Vinci, who epitomized the Renaissance man through his insatiable curiosity and learning. His diverse interests and relentless quest for knowledge led to groundbreaking achievements in art, science, and engineering. Learning new skills and knowledge contributes to self-improvement and personal fulfilment. For example, Sarah, a busy mother of two, decided to learn painting through online classes, which not only gave her a creative outlet but also boosted her confidence and sense of accomplishment. *In today's competitive job market, continuous learning provides a distinct advantage.* Consider the case of Mark, who transitioned from a traditional marketing role to a digital marketing expert by continuously updating his skills. His commitment to learning made him more attractive to employers and significantly increased his earning potential. Studies have shown that individuals who engage in lifelong learning tend to earn more over their careers. For instance, a report by the World Economic Forum highlighted that workers who continuously upgrade their skills are more likely to secure better-paying jobs and promotions. *Lifelong learning fosters critical thinking and innovation.* Steve Jobs, the co-founder of Apple, was a lifelong learner who constantly sought new knowledge and experiences. His innovative thinking revolutionized the tech industry and created products that changed the world. Howard Gardner's theory of multiple intelligences suggests that individuals have different kinds of intelligences. Lifelong learning allows individuals to develop these varied intelligences, leading to holistic growth and enhanced problem-solving abilities. Lifelong learning often involves engaging with like-minded individuals and building professional networks. For instance, Lisa joined a local coding bootcamp where she not only learned new programming skills but also connected with other tech enthusiasts, leading to collaborative projects and new career opportunities. Lifelong learners often become valuable contributors to their communities. Jane, a retired teacher, used her knowledge to volunteer at local schools, helping students with their studies and inspiring them to embrace learning. Her contributions have had a lasting impact on the community. *The journey of lifelong learning isn't just about personal growth; it's about inspiring others.* Nelson Mandela, an advocate for education, believed that "education is the most powerful weapon which you can use to change the world." His commitment to lifelong learning and education has inspired generations worldwide. Consider the legacy of Sir Isaac Newton, whose relentless pursuit of knowledge laid the foundation for modern physics. His contributions continue to inspire scientists and learners even centuries later. By embracing lifelong learning, we too can leave a legacy of knowledge and inspiration for future generations.

12

Continuous Learning and Skill Development

As a body is built of cells, and a house of bricks, so a man's mind is built of thoughts. The various characters of men are none other than compounds of thoughts of varying combinations.

The Importance of Lifelong Learning

1. **Adaptability to Change**

   o *Dynamic World:* The world is constantly evolving due to technological advancements, cultural shifts, and economic changes. Lifelong learning equips individuals with the skills and knowledge to adapt to these changes.
   o *Career Advancement*: Continuous learning enhances career prospects by keeping skills relevant and up-to-date. It opens up new opportunities for advancement and career shifts.

2. **Personal Growth and Fulfilment**

   o *Intellectual Stimulation*: Engaging in lifelong learning

stimulates the mind, fostering curiosity and intellectual growth. It keeps the brain active and promotes cognitive health.

- o *Self-Improvement*: Learning new skills and acquiring knowledge contributes to personal development. It boosts confidence, self-esteem, and a sense of accomplishment.

3. **Economic Benefits**

    - o *Competitive Edge:* In a competitive job market, continuous learning provides a competitive edge. It demonstrates a commitment to growth and adaptability, making individuals more attractive to employers.
    - o *Higher Earning Potential:* Advanced skills and knowledge often lead to higher earning potential. Lifelong learners are more likely to secure better-paying jobs and promotions.

4. **Enhanced Problem-Solving Skills**

    - o *Critical Thinking:* Lifelong learning develops critical thinking and problem-solving skills. It encourages individuals to approach challenges with an open and analytical mind.
    - o *Innovation*: Continuous learning fosters creativity and innovation. It exposes individuals to new ideas and perspectives, leading to innovative solutions and approaches.

5. **Social and Community Engagement**

    - o *Networking Opportunities:* Engaging in learning activities provides opportunities to connect with like-minded individuals and build professional networks.
    - o *Community Contribution:* Lifelong learners often

contribute positively to their communities by sharing knowledge, volunteering, and participating in civic activities.

Strategies for Continuous Skill Development

1. **Creating a Learning Plan**
    - *Identify Skills:* Identify the skills and knowledge areas you want to develop. This can be based on career goals, personal interests, or industry trends.
    - *Learning Resources:* Research and select appropriate learning resources, such as online courses, books, workshops, and mentorship programs.
    - *Schedule Learning:* Allocate regular time for learning activities. Consistency is key to making progress and integrating new knowledge.

2. **Leveraging Technology for Learning**
    - *Online Courses:* Enroll in online courses offered by platforms like Coursera, edX, Udemy, and LinkedIn Learning. These platforms offer a wide range of courses on various topics.
    - *Educational Apps:* Use educational apps like Duolingo for language learning, Khan Academy for foundational subjects, and Skillshare for creative skills.
    - *Podcasts and Webinars:* Listen to educational podcasts and attend webinars on topics of interest. These resources provide convenient ways to learn on the go.

3. **Engaging in Professional Development**
    - *Workshops and Seminars:* Attend workshops, seminars, and conferences to gain new insights and skills. These

events also provide networking opportunities.
- *Certifications*: Pursue professional certifications to validate your skills and enhance your resume. Certifications demonstrate commitment to continuous learning.
- *On-the-Job Training*: Take advantage of on-the-job training opportunities. Many organisations offer training programs to help employees develop new skills.

4. **Building a Learning Community**

   - *Study Groups:* Join or form study groups with peers who share similar learning goals. Collaborative learning fosters motivation and accountability.
   - *Mentorship*: Seek mentorship from experienced professionals who can provide guidance and support in your learning journey.
   - *Online Communities*: Participate in online communities and forums related to your field of interest. Engaging with a community of learners provides additional resources and perspectives.

5. **Developing Soft Skills**

   - *Communication Skills*: Improve communication skills through courses, workshops, and practice. Effective communication is essential for personal and professional success.
   - *Leadership Skills*: Develop leadership skills by taking on leadership roles, attending leadership training, and seeking feedback from mentors.
   - *Emotional Intelligence*: Enhance emotional intelligence through self-awareness exercises, mindfulness practices, and interpersonal skills training.

6. **Maintaining a Growth Mindset**

    o   ***Embrace Challenges:*** View challenges as opportunities to learn and grow. A growth mindset fosters resilience and adaptability.
    o   ***Seek Feedback:*** Actively seek feedback from peers, mentors, and supervisors. Constructive feedback provides valuable insights for improvement.
    o   ***Reflect on Learning:*** Regularly reflect on your learning experiences. Identify what worked well, what could be improved, and how to apply new knowledge.

Resources for Learning

1. **Online Learning Platforms**

    o   ***Coursera:*** Offers courses from top universities and institutions on a wide range of subjects. Courses often include video lectures, assignments, and peer discussions.
    o   ***edX:*** Provides access to courses from universities and organisations worldwide. edX courses cover various disciplines, including science, technology, humanities, and business.
    o   ***Udemy:*** Features a vast library of courses on diverse topics, created by industry experts. Udemy courses are often affordable and self-paced.
    o   ***LinkedIn Learning:*** Offers professional development courses in business, technology, and creative skills. LinkedIn Learning integrates with LinkedIn profiles, showcasing completed courses and skills.

2. **Educational Apps**

    o   ***Duolingo:*** A language learning app that offers interactive

lessons in multiple languages. Duolingo uses gamification to make learning fun and engaging.
- *Khan Academy:* Provides free educational resources on a wide range of subjects, including math, science, and humanities. Khan Academy is suitable for learners of all ages.
- *Skillshare*: Focuses on creative skills, offering courses in design, photography, writing, and more. Skillshare emphasizes project-based learning.

3. **Books and Publications**

- *Non-Fiction Books*: Read non-fiction books on topics of interest to gain in-depth knowledge. Books provide valuable insights and perspectives.
- *Academic Journals:* Access academic journals and publications in your field. Staying informed about the latest research and developments enhances expertise.
- *Magazines and Newsletters:* Subscribe to industry-specific magazines and newsletters to stay updated on trends, news, and best practices.

4. **Workshops and Conferences**

- *Industry Conferences*: Attend industry conferences to learn from experts, network with peers, and gain new insights. Conferences often feature keynote speakers, panel discussions, and workshops.
- *Local Workshops*: Participate in local workshops and seminars to develop specific skills. Community centres, libraries, and educational institutions often offer workshops on various topics.

5. Mentorship and Networking

- o *Professional Associations*: Join professional associations related to your field. These organisations often provide networking opportunities, resources, and mentorship programs.
- o *Alumni Networks*: Engage with alumni networks from your educational institutions. Alumni events and platforms offer opportunities to connect with professionals in your field.
- o *Social Media Groups*: Participate in social media groups and forums related to your interests. Platforms like LinkedIn, Reddit, and Facebook host groups for professionals and enthusiasts.

6. Podcasts and Webinars

- o *Educational Podcasts*: Listen to educational podcasts on topics of interest. Podcasts provide a convenient way to learn while commuting or exercising.
- o *Webinars:* Attend webinars hosted by experts and organisations. Webinars offer interactive learning experiences and opportunities to ask questions.

7. Formal Education

- o *Degree Programs:* Pursue degree programs to gain formal education and credentials. Universities and colleges offer undergraduate, graduate, and postgraduate programs.
- o *Continuing Education*: Enroll in continuing education programs to update skills and knowledge. Many institutions offer flexible options for working professionals.

Practical Applications of Continuous Learning

1. **In Personal Life**

    o *Lifelong Hobbies*: Develop hobbies that involve continuous learning, such as playing a musical instrument, painting, or gardening. These activities enhance creativity and relaxation.

    o *Personal Finance:* Educate yourself on personal finance to manage money effectively. Topics include budgeting, investing, and retirement planning.

    o *Health and Wellness:* Learn about health and wellness to maintain physical and mental well-being. Topics include nutrition, exercise, and stress management.

    o *Mindfulness Practices*: Incorporate mindfulness practices such as meditation and journaling to manage stress and enhance emotional resilience.

    o *Supportive Relationships:* Build and maintain supportive relationships with friends, family, and mentors who can provide encouragement and assistance during challenging times.

    o *Self-Compassion*: Practice self-compassion by being kind to yourself and acknowledging your efforts and progress. Self-compassion fosters resilience and reduces self-criticism.

2. **In Professional Life**

    o *Skill Development*: Identify and develop skills that are relevant to your career. This includes technical skills, soft skills, and industry-specific knowledge.

    o *Career Advancement:* Pursue learning opportunities that support career advancement. This includes

certifications, advanced degrees, and professional development courses.
- ○ ***Networking:*** Use learning activities as opportunities to network with peers and professionals. Building a strong professional network enhances career prospects.
- ○ ***Professional Development:*** Pursue continuous professional development to build skills and stay adaptable in a changing job market. This enhances career resilience and opportunities for advancement.
- ○ ***Mentorship Programs:*** Participate in mentorship programs to receive guidance and support from experienced professionals. Mentorship provides valuable insights and fosters resilience.

3. In Business and Entrepreneurship

- ○ ***Market Trends:*** Stay informed about market trends and industry developments. Continuous learning helps identify opportunities and adapt to changes.
- ○ ***Innovation:*** Foster a culture of innovation by encouraging continuous learning within your organisation. Support employees in their learning and development efforts.
- ○ ***Leadership Development:*** Invest in leadership development to build strong, effective leaders. This includes training, coaching, and mentorship programs.
- ○ ***Adaptation Strategies:*** Develop strategies for adapting to market changes and business challenges. This includes staying informed, being flexible, and continuously innovating.
- ○ ***Risk Management:*** Implement risk management practices to anticipate and mitigate potential obstacles.

This helps in maintaining business resilience and stability.

- o **_Resilient Leadership_**: Foster a culture of resilience within your organisation by promoting open communication, encouraging collaboration, and supporting employee well-being.

4. **In Education**

   - o **_Teaching Techniques:_** Educators should continuously update their teaching techniques and methodologies. This includes incorporating technology and innovative practices.
   - o **_Curriculum Development:_** Stay informed about educational trends and best practices. This helps in developing a relevant and effective curriculum.
   - o **_Student Engagement_**: Use continuous learning to enhance student engagement and success. Provide resources and support for students to pursue their learning goals.
   - o **_Student Resilience_**: Support student resilience by providing resources for mental health, stress management, and academic support. Encourage a growth mindset and perseverance.
   - o **_Teacher Well-being_**: Promote teacher well-being by offering professional development,

Continuous learning and skill development are essential for personal and professional success. By understanding the importance of lifelong learning, implementing effective strategies for skill development, and utilizing available resources, you can create a foundation for ongoing growth and achievement. Remember, just as a body is built of cells and a house of bricks, our minds and characters are shaped by the thoughts and knowledge we accumulate. Embrace the journey of continuous learning, and you will be well-equipped to navigate the complexities of life and achieve your goals.

13

Ethical Living and Social Responsibility

Perfect justice upholds the universe; perfect justice regulates human life and conduct.

Ethical living and social responsibility are foundational principles that guide personal and professional conduct, ensuring that our actions align with universal justice and fairness. These principles not only foster personal integrity but also contribute to the well-being of society. This chapter explores the importance of ethics in personal and professional life, the role of social responsibility and community involvement, and provides examples of ethical leaders who have made a significant impact.

The Importance of Ethics in Personal and Professional Life

1. **Building Trust and Credibility**

     o *Personal Integrity*: Ethical behaviour in personal life builds trust and credibility. Honesty, fairness, and transparency in interactions foster strong relationships and mutual respect.

     o *Professional Reputation*: In a professional context,

ethical conduct enhances reputation and credibility. Trustworthiness is a critical attribute for career advancement and professional success.

2. Guiding Decision-Making

- *Moral Compass:* Ethics serve as a moral compass, guiding decision-making processes. Ethical considerations ensure that decisions are made with integrity and respect for all stakeholders.
- *Consistency:* Adhering to ethical principles provides consistency in actions and decisions. This consistency builds reliability and fosters a stable environment.

3. Promoting Fairness and Justice

- *Equity:* Ethical living promotes fairness and equity, ensuring that everyone is treated justly. It addresses issues of inequality and discrimination, advocating for equal opportunities for all.
- *Accountability:* Ethics hold individuals accountable for their actions. This accountability encourages responsibility and transparency, preventing misconduct and corruption.

4. Enhancing Well-Being

- *Personal Fulfilment:* Living ethically contributes to personal fulfilment and peace of mind. It aligns actions with values, reducing internal conflicts and promoting a sense of purpose.
- *Workplace Culture:* In the workplace, ethical be enhances organisational culture. It fosters a positive environment where employees feel valued, respected, and motivated.

5. **Long-Term Success**

    o *Sustainable Practices*: Ethical practices contribute to long-term success and sustainability. They build loyal relationships, mitigate risks, and enhance the organisation's reputation.

    o *Resilience*: Ethics promote resilience by fostering trust and collaboration. Ethical organisations are better equipped to navigate challenges and crises.

Social Responsibility and Community Involvement

1. **Corporate Social Responsibility (CSR)**

    o CSR refers to the ethical obligation of businesses to contribute positively to society. It encompasses initiatives that promote environmental sustainability, social equity, and economic development.

    o *Benefits*: CSR enhances corporate reputation, builds consumer trust, and attracts and retains talent. It demonstrates a commitment to ethical practices and social welfare.

2. **Environmental Responsibility**

    o *Sustainable Practices*: Implementing sustainable practices, such as reducing carbon footprints, conserving resources, and promoting renewable energy, is a key aspect of social responsibility.

    o *Environmental Advocacy*: Supporting environmental causes and participating in conservation efforts contribute to the protection of natural resources and biodiversity.

3. **Social Equity**

    o *__Diversity and Inclusion__*: Promoting diversity and inclusion in the workplace and community ensures equal opportunities for all individuals, regardless of their background.

    o *__Social Justice Initiatives__*: Supporting social justice initiatives, such as education, healthcare, and housing for underserved communities, addresses systemic inequalities and improves quality of life.

4. **Community Engagement**

    o *__Volunteerism__*: Encouraging volunteerism and community service among employees and individuals fosters a sense of social responsibility and collective action.

    o *__Philanthropy__*: Contributing to charitable organisations and causes through donations and sponsorships supports community development and welfare.

5. **Ethical Consumerism**

    o *__Informed Choices__*: Making informed choices about products and services based on their ethical impact supports responsible businesses and promotes ethical practices.

    o *__Support for Ethical Brands__*: Supporting brands and companies that prioritise ethical practices, such as fair trade, cruelty-free, and environmentally friendly products, encourages ethical consumerism.

Examples of Ethical Leaders

1. Nelson Mandela

- *Background*: Nelson Mandela, the former President of South Africa, is renowned for his leadership in the fight against apartheid and his commitment to justice and equality.
- *Ethical Leadership*: Mandela's ethical leadership was evident in his dedication to non-violent resistance, reconciliation, and the promotion of human rights.
- *Impact*: His efforts led to the dismantling of apartheid, the establishment of a multiracial democracy in South Africa, and global recognition of the importance of justice and equality.

2. Mahatma Gandhi

- *Background*: Mahatma Gandhi, the leader of the Indian independence movement, is celebrated for his principles of non-violence (ahimsa) and truth (satyagraha).
- *Ethical Leadership*: Gandhi's ethical leadership was characterised by his commitment to non-violent civil disobedience, social justice, and self-reliance.
- *Impact*: Gandhi's leadership contributed to India's independence, inspired civil rights movements worldwide, and emphasized the power of ethical conduct in achieving social change.

3. Mother Teresa

- *Background*: Mother Teresa, the founder of the Missionaries of Charity, is known for her humanitarian work and dedication to helping the poor and marginalized.

- ***Ethical Leadership***: Mother Teresa's ethical leadership was marked by her compassion, selflessness, and unwavering commitment to serving those in need.
- ***Impact***: Her work provided care and support to countless individuals, earned her the Nobel Peace Prize, and highlighted the importance of empathy and service.

4. Dr. Martin Luther King Jr.

- ***Background***: Dr. Martin Luther King Jr., a leader in the American civil rights movement, is remembered for his advocacy for racial equality and non-violent protest.
- ***Ethical Leadership***: King's ethical leadership was demonstrated through his commitment to justice, equality, and non-violence, as well as his powerful oratory and vision of a just society.
- ***Impact***: His leadership played a pivotal role in the passage of civil rights legislation, advanced the cause of racial equality, and inspired movements for social justice globally.

5. Jane Goodall

- ***Background***: Dr. Jane Goodall, a primatologist and conservationist, is renowned for her groundbreaking research on chimpanzees and her advocacy for environmental conservation.
- ***Ethical Leadership***: Goodall's ethical leadership is reflected in her dedication to scientific integrity, animal welfare, and environmental sustainability.
- ***Impact***: Her work has advanced our understanding of primates, promoted conservation efforts worldwide, and raised awareness about the interconnectedness of all life.

Practical Applications of Ethical Living and Social Responsibility

1. **In Personal Life**

   o *Ethical Decision-Making*: Apply ethical principles in daily decision-making. Consider the impact of your actions on others and strive to act with integrity and fairness.

   o *Community Involvement*: Get involved in community activities and volunteer for causes you are passionate about. Community involvement fosters a sense of social responsibility and collective action.

   o *Sustainable Living:* Adopt sustainable living practices, such as reducing waste, conserving energy, and supporting eco-friendly products. Small changes in daily habits can have a significant positive impact on the environment.

2. **In Professional Life**

   o *Ethical Workplace Culture:* Promote an ethical workplace culture by leading by example, encouraging open communication, and upholding ethical standards.

   o *Corporate Social Responsibility:* Advocate for and participate in CSR initiatives within your organisation. Support programs that address social, environmental, and economic issues.

   o *Professional Integrity*: Maintain professional integrity by adhering to ethical guidelines, being transparent in your dealings, and holding yourself accountable for your actions.

3. **In Business and Entrepreneurship**

    o *Ethical Business Practices:* Implement ethical business practices, such as fair labor policies, transparent supply chains, and responsible marketing. Ethical practices build trust and loyalty among consumers and stakeholders.

    o *Sustainable Business Models:* Develop sustainable business models that prioritise environmental stewardship, social equity, and economic viability.

    o *Philanthropy and Community Support:* Engage in philanthropy and support community development initiatives. Businesses have a unique opportunity to make a positive impact on society.

4. **In Education**

    o *Ethics Education:* Integrate ethics education into the curriculum to teach students the importance of ethical behaviour and social responsibility.

    o **Role Modelling:** Educators should serve as role models of ethical behaviour, demonstrating integrity, fairness, and compassion in their interactions with students.

    o *Service Learning:* Encourage service learning and community engagement projects that allow students to apply ethical principles and contribute to society.

Final Thoughts

Ethical living and social responsibility are essential components of a just and fair society. By understanding the importance of ethics in personal and professional life, engaging in social responsibility and community involvement, and learning from the examples of ethical leaders, we can foster a culture of integrity, fairness, and compassion. Perfect justice, as a guiding principle, ensures that our actions align with universal fairness and contribute positively to the world around us. Embrace these principles, and you will be well-equipped to lead a life of ethical integrity and social responsibility.

14

Creating a Legacy

It is the culmination of actions, values, and contributions that shape how an individual is remembered and how their influence continues to benefit future generations.

Leaving a legacy is about making a lasting impact that endures beyond one's lifetime This chapter delves into the meaning of leaving a legacy, outlines steps to create a meaningful legacy, and shares inspirational stories of individuals whose legacies have had a profound impact.

What It Means to Leave a Legacy

1. **Definition of Legacy**
    - ***Enduring Impact:*** A legacy is the lasting influence and contributions that an individual leaves behind. It encompasses achievements, values, and the positive changes they have made.
    - ***Cultural and Social Influence:*** Legacies shape cultural and social landscapes, influencing how societies evolve and remember past contributions.

2. **Personal and Professional Legacy**

    o *Personal Legacy:* Personal legacies involve the values, ethics, and relationships that define an individual's life. It includes how one is remembered by family, friends, and the community.

    o *Professional Legacy:* Professional legacies are built through career achievements, mentorship, and contributions to one's field. It includes the impact on colleagues, industry standards, and advancements.

3. **Components of a Legacy**

    o *Values and Principles:* Core values and principles that guide actions and decisions form the foundation of a legacy. Integrity, compassion, and dedication are often key components.

    o *Achievements and Contributions:* Tangible achievements and contributions, such as innovations, charitable work, and leadership roles, are critical aspects of a legacy.

    o *Influence on Others:* The influence on others through mentorship, inspiration, and guidance significantly shapes one's legacy. It includes how others carry forward the lessons and values imparted.

4. **Significance of a Legacy**

    o *Inspiration for Future Generations:* A meaningful legacy inspires future generations to pursue their goals and uphold the values demonstrated by the individual.

    o **Continuity of Positive Impact:** Legacies ensure the continuity of positive impact, promoting sustained progress and improvement in various aspects of life and society.

Steps to Create a Meaningful Legacy

1. Define Your Values and Vision

- *Identify Core Values:* Reflect on and identify the core values that define your character and guide your actions. These values form the foundation of your legacy.
- *Articulate Your Vision:* Develop a clear vision of the impact you want to leave behind. Consider the areas where you want to make a difference and the legacy you wish to create.

2. Set Long-Term Goals

- *Strategic Planning:* Set long-term goals that align with your vision and values. Develop a strategic plan outlining the steps needed to achieve these goals.
- *Milestones and Benchmarks:* Establish milestones and benchmarks to track progress. Regularly review and adjust your goals to stay aligned with your legacy vision.

3. Make a Positive Impact

- *Community Involvement:* Engage in community involvement and volunteer work to make a positive impact. Contribute to causes and organisations that align with your values.
- *Mentorship and Guidance:* Provide mentorship and guidance to others. Share your knowledge, experiences, and values to inspire and support their growth.

4. Pursue Excellence in Your Field

- *Professional Achievements:* Strive for excellence in your professional field. Achieve significant milestones,

contribute to advancements, and set high standards.
- o **Continuous Learning:** Commit to continuous learning and skill development. Stay informed about industry trends and innovations to maintain relevance and expertise.

5. **Foster Relationships and Connections**
   - o **Build Strong Relationships:** Build and maintain strong relationships with family, friends, colleagues, and community members. Positive relationships enhance your influence and impact.
   - o **Network and Collaborate:** Network and collaborate with like-minded individuals and organisations. Partnerships amplify your efforts and extend your legacy.

6. **Document and Share Your Journey**
   - o **Writing and Speaking:** Document your journey through writing and speaking engagements. Share your experiences, insights, and lessons learned with a broader audience.
   - o **Publications and Media:** Publish books, articles, and multimedia content that encapsulate your values and contributions. Use media platforms to reach and inspire others.

7. **Establish Foundations and Endowments**
   - o **Charitable Foundations:** Establish charitable foundations and endowments to support causes that align with your values. Ensure the continuity of your contributions through organised efforts.
   - o **Scholarships and Grants:** Create scholarships and grants to support education and innovation. These

initiatives provide opportunities for future generations to excel.

8. **Lead by Example**

   o *Model Ethical Behaviour:* Lead by example by consistently demonstrating ethical behaviour and integrity. Your actions set a standard for others to follow.
   o *Inspire and Motivate*: Inspire and motivate others through your dedication, perseverance, and commitment to your vision. Show that making a meaningful impact is achievable.

Inspirational Legacy Stories

1. **Marie Curie**

   o *Background*: Marie Curie was a pioneering scientist known for her groundbreaking research on radioactivity. She was the first woman to win a Nobel Prize and remains the only person to win Nobel Prizes in two different scientific fields.
   o *Legacy*: Curie's legacy is one of scientific excellence, innovation, and dedication to research. Her discoveries have had a lasting impact on science and medicine.
   o *Impact*: Curie's legacy inspires women in science and highlights the importance of perseverance, curiosity, and dedication to advancing knowledge.

2. **Martin Luther King Jr.**

   o *Background*: Dr. Martin Luther King Jr. was a leader in the American civil rights movement, known for his advocacy for racial equality and non-violent protest.
   o *Legacy*: King's legacy is characterised by his commitment

to justice, equality, and non-violence. His leadership played a pivotal role in advancing civil rights in the United States.

- o ***Impact:*** King's legacy continues to inspire movements for social justice and equality worldwide. His speeches, writings, and actions remain a powerful source of inspiration.

3. Mother Teresa

- o ***Background:*** Mother Teresa, founder of the Missionaries of Charity, dedicated her life to helping the poor and marginalized.
- o ***Legacy:*** Mother Teresa's legacy is one of compassion, selflessness, and unwavering commitment to serving those in need. Her humanitarian work has had a profound impact on countless lives.
- o ***Impact:*** Her legacy continues through the Missionaries of Charity and serves as a testament to the power of empathy, service, and dedication to others.

4. Mahatma Gandhi

- o ***Background:*** Mahatma Gandhi, leader of the Indian independence movement, is renowned for his principles of non-violence and truth.
- o ***Legacy:*** Gandhi's legacy is one of non-violent resistance, social justice, and commitment to truth. His leadership inspired movements for civil rights and freedom across the globe.
- o ***Impact:*** Gandhi's legacy continues to influence global movements for peace and justice. His philosophy and methods remain relevant and inspiring.

Practical Applications of Creating a Legacy

1. **In Personal Life**

    o *Family Values*: Instill strong values and principles within your family. Share your experiences and wisdom to guide future generations.

    o *Personal Achievements:* Pursue personal achievements that reflect your values and passions. Celebrate milestones and reflect on their significance.

    o *Community Involvement*: Engage in community service and volunteer work. Make a positive impact on your community through active participation and support.

2. **In Professional Life**

    o *Career Excellence*: Strive for excellence in your professional career. Achieve significant milestones and contribute to advancements in your field.

    o *Mentorship:* Mentor and support colleagues and aspiring professionals. Share your knowledge and experiences to guide their growth and development.

    o *Ethical Leadership*: Demonstrate ethical leadership in your professional conduct. Uphold integrity, fairness, and transparency in all your actions.

3. **In Business and Entrepreneurship**

    o *Innovative Contributions*: Contribute innovative ideas and solutions that advance your industry. Create products and services that make a positive impact.

    o *Corporate Responsibility*: Implement corporate social responsibility initiatives that benefit society. Support

causes and organisations that align with your values.
- o ***Business Legacy:*** Build a business that reflects your values and principles. Ensure its long-term sustainability and positive impact.

4. **In Education**
   - o ***Educational Contributions:*** Contribute to the field of education through teaching, research, and publications. Share your knowledge to inspire and educate others.
   - o ***Student Support:*** Support students through scholarships, mentorship, and guidance. Help them achieve their educational and career goals.
   - o ***Community Engagement:*** Engage with the educational community through workshops, seminars, and collaborations. Promote continuous learning and development.

Establishing a legacy entails leaving a lasting impact that extends beyond one's lifetime. By understanding the meaning of leaving a legacy, taking steps to create a meaningful legacy, and drawing inspiration from the legacies of others, we can shape a future that reflects our values, achievements, and contributions. Remember, the good man who is overtaken with calamity today is reaping the result of his former evil sowing; later he will reap the happy result of his present good sowing. Embrace the journey of creating a legacy, and you will leave behind a lasting influence that inspires and benefits future generations.

Final Thoughts

As we conclude this journey, it's essential to reflect on the transformative power of the principles and practices we've explored. The art of Futuresmithing is not just about planning and achieving goals; it's about shaping a life that is rich in purpose, fulfilment, and positive impact. Here are some final thoughts and motivational insights to inspire you as you continue your journey:

1. **Embrace Your Unique Path**

   o *Individuality*: Recognize that your path is unique. Embrace your strengths, passions, and experiences as you forge your way forward.
   o *Authenticity*: Stay true to yourself and your values. Authenticity is the foundation of a meaningful and impactful life.

2. **Persevere Through Challenges**

   o *Resilience*: Develop resilience to navigate obstacles and setbacks. Every challenge is an opportunity to learn and grow stronger.
   o *Determination*: Maintain unwavering determination and commitment to your goals. Persistence is key to overcoming adversity and achieving success.

3. **Inspire and Empower Others**

   o *Mentorship*: Share your knowledge and experiences to mentor and inspire others. Empowering others amplifies your impact and creates a ripple effect of positive change.
   o *Community Engagement*: Engage with your community and contribute to collective well-being. Collaboration and support strengthen the fabric of society.

4. **Cultivate a Growth Mindset**

   o *Lifelong Learning*: Commit to lifelong learning and continuous improvement. Stay curious and open to new

experiences and knowledge.
- ○ ***Adaptability***: Embrace change and adaptability as essential components of growth. Flexibility allows you to thrive in dynamic environments.

5. **Balance Ambition with Well-Being**

    - ○ ***Holistic Approach***: Balance your ambition and goals with holistic well-being. Prioritise physical, mental, and emotional health to sustain long-term success.
    - ○ ***Mindfulness***: Practice mindfulness and self-care to maintain balance and inner peace. A well-balanced life enhances productivity and fulfilment.

6. **Leave a Lasting Legacy**

    - ○ ***Impact***: Focus on the impact you want to leave behind. Your legacy is defined by the positive changes you create and the lives you touch.
    - ○ ***Values***: Uphold your core values in all your actions and decisions. Integrity and compassion are the cornerstones of a meaningful legacy.

Call to Action for Readers

As you embark on your journey as a Futuresmith, remember that the power to shape your future lies within you. Here are some actionable steps to help you put the principles and practices from this book into action:

1. **Develop Productive Habits**

    - ○ ***Daily Routine***: Establish a daily routine that includes habits promoting health, productivity, and personal growth. Consistency is key to building lasting habits.

- ○ ***Continuous Improvement:*** Regularly review and refine your habits. Seek opportunities for continuous improvement and growth.

2. **Build Strong Relationships**

   - ○ ***Networking:*** Actively build and maintain strong personal and professional relationships. Engage in meaningful interactions and offer support to others.
   - ○ ***Mentorship:*** Seek mentorship from experienced individuals and offer mentorship to those who can benefit from your guidance.

3. **Leverage Technology Wisely**

   - ○ ***Productivity Tools:*** Utilize technology tools and apps to enhance efficiency and productivity. Ensure a balanced approach to avoid digital burnout.
   - ○ ***Continuous Learning:*** Take advantage of online learning platforms and resources to stay informed and develop new skills.

4. **Prioritise Health and Well-Being**

   - ○ ***Physical Activity:*** Incorporate regular physical activity into your routine. Exercise supports physical health and mental well-being.
   - ○ ***Mental Wellness:*** Practice mindfulness and stress management techniques to maintain emotional balance. Prioritise sleep, nutrition, and self-care.

5. **Contribute to Society**

   - ○ ***Community Involvement:*** Engage in community service and volunteer work. Make a positive impact on society through active participation.

o ***Ethical Practices:*** Uphold ethical standards in all your actions. Promote social responsibility and contribute to causes that align with your values.

6. **Reflect and Adapt**

   o ***Regular Reflection:*** Take time to reflect on your progress and experiences. Identify areas for improvement and celebrate achievements.
   o ***Adaptability:*** Stay flexible and open to change. Adapt your plans and strategies based on new insights and evolving circumstances.

Manifesto: Embrace Your Role as a Futuresmith

As a Futuresmith, you have the power to shape your destiny and leave a lasting impact. Embrace this journey with passion, resilience, and unwavering commitment to your values. By integrating the principles and practices outlined in this book, you will build a future that is not only successful but also meaningful and fulfilling.

- Lead with Integrity: Uphold integrity in all your endeavours. Ethical conduct is the foundation of trust and credibility.
- Pursue Excellence: Strive for excellence in every aspect of your life. Continuous improvement and dedication to your goals will propel you forward.
- Cultivate Resilience: Develop resilience to navigate challenges and setbacks. Every obstacle is an opportunity for growth and learning.
- Make a Positive Impact: Focus on making a positive impact on your community and the world. Your legacy is defined by the difference you make in the lives of others.

Embrace your role as a Futuresmith and embark on this journey with confidence and determination. The future you build today will shape the world of tomorrow. Take action, stay committed, and make your mark on the world.